# The Voices of God

the

# Voices of God

## Hearing God in the silence

# Charles R. Lanham

A Deacon's Corner Book
Deacon's Corner Publications
Reno, Nevada

All scriptural quotations are taken from the Saint Joseph Edition of The New American Bible, Catholic Book Publishing Corp., New York (1970).

Cover Design by C. R. Lanham

ISBN-13: 978-0-9905582-0-0
ISBN-10: 0990558207




Published by Deacon's Corner Publications
Reno, Nevada 89519

Printed and bound in the United States of America.

# Dedication

With great love
to the parishioners of

**Saint Albert the Great Catholic Community**

*There is a reason and a purpose,*
*within each moment that we live;*
*as we pass through every season*
*God calls us all to give*
*our love to all His creatures,*
*His creatures great and small.*
*Know the love of God and neighbor*
*is the greatest love of all.*

— CRL

# Contents

# Preface

Every life has a beginning, a middle, and a future. There can be no end, for we have been assured by none other than God Himself and confirmed by His only Son, that we will be resurrected from the dead and will, depending upon how well we have exercised our free will during our earthly existence, either spend eternity with him in heaven or be banished from God's sight forever. Either way, life will go on and on and on, for some just not as pleasant an eternity as they had expected or had hoped.

God has made it abundantly clear that He loves all of His creation, and ardently desires that we spend all eternity with Him. And Jesus told us through his disciples, *"In my Father's house there are many dwelling places. If there were not, would I have told you that I am going to prepare a place for you?"*[1]

Although Jesus assured us that a dwelling place in heaven has been prepared for you, it is neither automatically

---

[1] Jn 14:2

obtained nor free. You must pay a price to be admitted: you must have faith in God and in His Son, and you must obey God's commandments.

During the final year of Diaconate Formation, I was offered the opportunity to write an 'occasional' column for our parish's weekly bulletin under the heading of Deacon's Corner and I jumped at it. My mother was an award-winning journalist and a writer, and although I inherited much of her passion for the written word, making a living had kept my muse on the backburner for entirely too long.

The occasional column almost instantly developed into regular weekly contributions now exceeding 140 reflections on faith, hope, love, our relationship with God, and His relationship with us, along with anything that the Holy Spirit wanted me to say.

I do not make that last statement lightly or in jest. Columnists work under a deadline and mine is no later than noon Wednesdays. Each week, perhaps more weeks than not, I find myself at a complete loss for words, the brain simply refusing to engage. And invariably two hours before deadline with my brain completely shut down, my fingers begin to type out 550 words of something.

I cannot tell you how many times I have found myself reading for the first time a completed column that had been written by the ten fingers attached to my own two hands. The author could only have been the Holy Spirit, for I find myself reading what has been written with new eyes.

The genesis for this book came about during our initial diaconate retreat some seven years ago. The first reading for the day was from 1 Kings, which recalled the occasion when the LORD commanded Elijah to go out of the cave because the LORD would be passing by. And as Elijah stood at its entrance, a strong wind, earthquake, and fire came but the LORD was not in any of them. But the LORD was in a tiny whispering sound and it was then that Elijah heard the voice of the LORD.[2] I realized that I had been hearing that tiny whispering sound of the LORD speaking to me for all of my life.

During a period of silent reflection, I found myself writing what can now be found in the first few pages of Chapter Four and taking the initial steps on what has become a rather tortuous and often unexpected journey, the outcome of which you now hold in your hands, and to which I have given the title The Voices of God.

Admittedly, and to provide you the reader with full disclosure, a significant part of this book has been included from my aforementioned weekly columns. I have done so for two specific reasons: first, many of the readers of my weekly column have requested that I put them into book form, and second, because I found their content was both appropriate and

_____

[2] 1 Kgs 19:9a, 11-13a

directly pertinent to the purpose and subject matter that I was attempting to put to paper.

While the columns that I have chosen to include may appear familiar to those who have previously read them when first published in the bulletin, I have greatly expanded and amended much of the original, given the opportunity to go well beyond the limited number of words for that much smaller publication.

Lest you, dear reader, have now come to believe that this book is a mere regurgitation of the familiar, let me assure you that there is much that is new, previously unpublished work, especially in most of the later chapters.

While my intent and primary aim in writing this book has been to outline and illustrate the infinite voices (methods and means) whereby God chooses to communicate with His creations, especially when it concerns humanity, it also contains much of a personal journal that, in some sense, chronicles my own personal journey of faith. I could have easily and justifiably given it the title HERE AND BACK AGAIN, but unfortunately, that title is no longer available, thanks to Bilbo Baggins né J. R. R. Tolkien[3].

To put it plainly, I am a Revert, a cradle Catholic who lost his way and his faith sometime around the age of eighteen. Like Augustine, I plunged into the lovely things which God had

---

[3] **Here and Back Again** is the title of the book written by Bilbo Baggins, the protagonist in J. R. R. Tolkien's classic tale of Middle Earth **The Hobbit** and subsequently included in his trilogy **The Lord of the Rings**.

created, and likewise, those created things kept me away from Him for over thirty years. And yet, like many of my generation, I never ceased categorizing myself as Catholic.

I simply walked away, leaving the detritus of my faith crumbling in the dust of some forgotten corner of my mind and shelving my personal relationship with God for another time. I was far too busy with living the good life to spend any time living with God.

Fortunately, God was never so busy that He forgot about me nor too busy to pay attention to my needs no matter how much I ignored His voices.

Deacon Chuck Lanham
Reno, Nevada
2014

# Acknowledgements

It is with the deepest devotion and gratitude that I begin by acknowledging the Source and Creator of all things. For without God and His infinite love, all of creation – and with absolute certainty, this book – would simply not exist. I am especially grateful for His patience, forgiveness, love, and persistence in waiting for this poor sinful creature to finally come to his senses.

Without the steadfast love, support, and prayers of my wife Janet, who has ever walked beside me through my self-imposed exile in the desert and the valley of death for over forty-six years, I could never have entered the Promised Land. I can only say that you are truly a saint and I have and will always love you.

I was brought into this world through the love of my parents, Bob and Nellie Ann Lanham. They raised me, nurtured me, and loved me, but above all they gifted me with the example of what true devotion and love ought to be.

My father taught me how the poor in spirit shall see God. He taught me how to love and honor another. He taught me what it meant always to do your best while focusing on the needs of others.

My mother taught me how the meek shall inherit the earth. She taught me the power and wonder of the written word and how to use it as a voice for good.

Above all, they both taught me faith. They lived it, breathed it, and tried their utmost to be true examples of Christ in all that they said and did. I think of them every day and miss them terribly.

God works His marvelous deeds in many ways and it is often through the lives of others that He speaks to us so clearly. My journey back to Him began when I first visited my cousin Vicki Fach and her husband Wes along with their growing family for it was an unforgettable religious experience that truly humbled and inspired me. Their faith and love has renewed my spirit and lifted my soul to God.

I initially developed the idea for this book many years ago but never traveled farther than a few paragraphs before allowing the idea to languish in a long forgotten file on my computer. Fortunately, I had a great friend in Ron Reigle, who encouraged me, rather insistently as I recall, to pick up the pen and complete the book. I will be forever in your debt my friend. Thank you.

I have discovered that the writing is only the first step in the journey an author must travel to ever reach publication. Without the help and creative talents of others, this book would surely have been stillborn. Fortunately, I was blessed to have been introduced to Full Quiver Publishing, and its owners James & Ellen Hrkach, who were instrumental in bringing this book to life. As an experienced author and publisher of multiple books that promote the Catholic Church's teachings on sexuality and marriage, Ellen encouraged and coached me through the publishing labyrinth and made the intractable doable. She also lifted up my spirit and gave me the strength to see it through to the end. James provided his creative genius to the cover, which is no small task. Thank you both for all that you have done.

I would be remiss if I failed to acknowledge the debt I owe to my friend, neighbor, and spiritual director, Monique Jacobs. Your patience, forbearance, wisdom, and counsel have kept this often lost soul on the right path. Thank you for always being there.

Several priests, whom I consider both mentors and friends, deserve special mention, for they each have helped in their own unique way in my faith journey and the completion of this book.

I am deeply indebted to Father Bob Simpson who patiently listened to my desert story and guided me upon my return. You are a very special man and have my everlasting gratitude for being there when I was in need.

Father Mike Mahone gave me the gift of his support and guidance before, during, and after my formative years toward the permanent diaconate. Thank you for being there and believing.

Father Mark Hanifan first gave me the opportunity to write and brought the Deacon's Corner to the bulletin. His support, encouragement, and guidance have been a blessing and I am very grateful for everything you have done.

A late entry into my life, Father Honesto Agustin has been a true inspiration, a wonderful friend and mentor. The pure joy and exuberance for life that you demonstrate toward everyone, along with your genuine gift of caring for the needs of others, have made all of us who know you better souls. Your knowledge and counsel in all things biblical have been immensely helpful and I am deeply in your debt.

Above all, I wish to thank the countless individuals through whom God has spoken to me over the years. You almost certainly do not know who you are for you were never aware of Him at the time, but I assure you, He was there and I heard His voice in you.

God bless you all.

# Introduction

*Ask and it will be given to you;*
*seek and you will find;*
*knock and the door will be opened to you.*
*For everyone who asks, receives;*
*and the one who seeks, finds;*
*and to the one who knocks,*
*the door will be opened.*

Matt 7:7-8

A common complaint from many is that God never speaks to them. They pray, they argue, they plead, but God never responds. Fortunately, their complaint, while common enough couldn't be further from the truth. The truth is that God responds to every prayer, every request, and every cry or plea for help.

The problem is not on God's end. The problem is one that lies squarely on our own two shoulders, for we have forgotten how to listen for His Voice — or more precisely His Voices — and as a result we have lost the ability to hear and discern what He is trying to tell us.

He created us in His image and likeness, and bestowed on us free will, a notion that, to our great detriment, we have all too often taken as an unrestricted license to do all that we desire rather than what is the right and good thing to do, what God desires for us to do.

Man's concupiscence, his inclination to sin, began almost before he took his first breath. Ignoring for the moment the serious damage that sin does to our souls and to our relationship with God we must also consider how it affects our spiritual hearing. Every time we sin, we do damage to the spiritual cochlea of our soul. Our ability to hear the tiny whispering sound of the LORD is diminished by the ever increasing, overwhelming noise of sin.

The good news is that, unlike the physical damage to our ears which often results in permanent loss of hearing, we can almost always regain any loss of spiritual hearing. Certainly not without serious effort and persistence but with God's grace and the will to build a close, personal relationship with Him, anyone, no matter how much the sinner, can once again hear God's Voice.

Every now and then, I come across a word or phrase that surprises me. Although familiar, something new presents itself and I have to pause and reflect on the difference. Not too long ago during a period of quiet reflection, my mind was suddenly filled with the phrase *"Ask and it will be given; seek and you will find; knock and it will be opened to you."*[4]

As I reflected on its meaning, I suddenly saw something new in the passage, something that I had never discerned before. While it was quite honestly rather trite and embarrassingly unimportant, I realized that the first letter of the first word of each phrase spelled the word ASK. While I am perfectly aware that this discovery is of no real or practical importance, it did cause me to more deeply reflect on these words of our LORD and Savior.

Upon reflection, I concluded that each phrase calls us to act; we must actively and purposefully engage in some action: Ask, Seek, and Knock. Without action there can be no reaction, no consequent response. In addition, each act requires that we condition ourselves and prepare ourselves in some manner for the response from God.

---

[4] Lk 11:9, Mt 7:7

What followed from my reflection has become the general structure for this book. I have divided it into three parts, each part corresponding to the need to ask, seek, and knock.

## Part I: Ask and it will be given to you

**When you ask, you must listen.** As I learned once during a retreat, to pray you must *"sit down and shut up,"* although I personally prefer *"Be still, and know that I Am God."*[5] All of your senses must be tuned to hear God's voice. Remember that God speaks to us in many ways; not necessarily as you might expect and often not with words.

## Part II: Seek and you will find

**When you seek, you must open your eyes, your mind, and your soul.** You must shine the light of Christ within in order to discover the unseen and the hidden. You cannot find what you seek in the darkness. Equally important is the necessity to empty yourself of any vestiges of sin. For sin hides the light and darkens the soul.

## Part III: Knock, and the door will open

**When you knock, you must enter and embrace the unknown and the unknowable.** You must put aside your fears

---

[5] Ps 46:10

of what lies beyond, knock down the walls of separation, distrust, hatred, and fear. You must accept and embrace what is now unknown to you because it is and it will be of God.

The moments of our lives lie unknown before we live them for the future hides beneath the horizon of what is yet to be. We cannot hope to live them, enjoy them, and embrace them unless we choose to act. To live truly we must ask, seek, and knock. God will always respond. All we have to do is ASK.

# The Voices of God

# Part 1

Ask and it will be given to you

# Thank You

*Thank You most loving Father,*
*    for all the beauty which You have created.*
*Thank You for this life which You have given*
*    and all the gifts You have bestowed.*
*Thank You for Your touch, Your caress,*
*    Your tender love and watchfulness.*
*Thank You for listening to one so unworthy,*
*    please grant me the grace of silence,*
*the gift of solitude, and the serenity of stillness*
*    so that I may always hear Your Voice.*

# Chapter One

## Be still and know that I am God

*Come and see the works of the LORD,*
*who has done fearsome deeds on earth;*
*Who stops wars to the ends of the earth,*
*breaks the bow, splinters the spear,*
*and burns the shields with fire;*
*Be still and know that I am God!*
*I am exalted among the nations,*
*exalted on the earth.*

Psalm 46:9-11

# Silence, solitude, and stillness

In order to nurture and grow in a deep intimate relationship with God, to be in His Presence and to hear His Voice, one must embrace the journey through the cathedrals of silence, solitude, and stillness.

## Silence

To be silent is to *breathe in* quiet moments. You cannot *breathe in* and speak at the same time. To speak you must breathe out, thus breaking the silence. You must be silent in order to *breathe in* the Breath of God. You must be silent to hear His Voice.

## Solitude

God speaks to every soul in solitude, in one's aloneness with Him. What God has to say to you is deeply intimate and always personal. You cannot hear God as long as you are completely consumed by the noise of living and the distractions that come from earthly things.

## Stillness

You must empty yourself of the world and all its enticements and *"be still"* to know and hear God. It is only in the stillness of your being that you will sense His presence. Empty your mind of thought, quiet the beating of your heart, and clean the sanctuary of your soul. Let go of all that is not God and let Him enter your soul.

# Silence is golden

Undoubtedly, most of us have either heard or used the phrase *"silence is golden"* at some point in our life. This is actually the final refrain of an old Swiss inscription *"Sprecfien ist silbern, Schweigen ist golden"*[6] which in English translates to *"Speech is silver, Silence is golden."*

We often have a tendency to speak in haste, immediately opening our mouths, responding with little or no thought to what we have just heard. More often than not then what we utter makes us look foolish. It would have been far wiser to have kept silent. The 19th century poet Thomas Carlyle once wrote that *"Silence is the element in which great things fashion themselves together; that at length they may emerge, full-formed and majestic, into the daylight of life, which they are thenceforth to rule."*[7]

The problem with breaking silence is that words once spoken can never be unsaid. Right or wrong, good or bad, when we speak, our words become etched in the memories of those who hear them; they become the image of you in their minds.

---

[6] Unknown author, Old Swiss inscription.
[7] Thomas Carlyle, *Sartor Resartus*, 1834

Golda Meir, the former prime minister of Israel, knew the virtue of silence. Elinor Burkett, author of GOLDA[8] tells how often people who met her were impressed with her intellect and wisdom. Upon reflection, those who spent any time with Golda came to realize that she asked questions and then listened intently, focused completely on the other person. She kept her own views to herself, and it was her silence that increased her stature in the eyes of others.

When we speak, we cannot contemplate, and without contemplation, we cannot be present to the silent world that surrounds us. Too often we attempt to fill quiet moments with words because we are uncomfortable with the silence that pervades. When we speak to fill the void, it is an attempt to control the situation, to become the master of the moment. *"I am master of all I explain,"*[9] someone once said. *"Where one cannot understand without words, no amount of explanation will make things clear,"*[10] wrote Myrtle Reed.

It is in silence that we come into the presence of God and it is only in silence that we can hear His Voice. As Elijah experienced, the LORD was not in the great and strong wind, earthquake, or fire. The LORD was in a tiny whispering sound. For us to hear the Voice of God, we must remain silent, we must listen intently, and we must focus everything on Him. We will

---

[8] Elinor Burkett, *Golda*, June 30, 2009
[9] Anonymous
[10] Myrtle Reed, *The Master's Violin*, 1904

never hear His voice as long as we breathe out, as long as we insist on speaking.

"*Sprecfien ist silbern.*" Speech is silver. Speak and you will hear and know only the sound of your own voice. "*Schweigen ist golden.*" Silence is golden. Be silent and listen and you will hear the Voice of God.

## The intimacy of silence

We have been created by an all-loving, all-knowing God; an unknowable Creator who loves us beyond all knowing. For us to be in an intimate relationship with God, we must be silent.

Silence provides us with an opportunity to attain a deeper intimacy with others, with ourselves, and with God. Silence is the ultimate language of love. It is a communion of kindred spirits, a covenantal acknowledgement of intense devotion.

Our culture, biased and skewed by much of the popular media, has long promoted the notion that intimate relationships are physically noisy affairs, filled with perspiration and passion. Nothing could be further from the truth. Like magic, this image of intimacy is nothing but a pale illusion and a false dream.

True intimacy in any spousal relationship is much deeper and far more complex. It requires a person to give of one's self completely to another as the following excerpt so aptly describes:

> *What does it feel like? Imagine a married couple sitting together on the front porch of their home. They are together, but hardly a word passes between them. They are simply enjoying being together; that's all it takes to make them happy. Perhaps they are holding hands, perhaps not. The look in their eyes is one of peace, contentment, and satisfaction. They know each other's weaknesses, flaws, and annoying habits, but none of that matters at this moment. Their love covers all of them. Sometimes a full hour can pass while they sit together, but the couple doesn't care. They have lost track of time.*[11]

Once during a confirmation class, I told my students that the closer and more intimate a relationship, the fewer words must be spoken. The more you must speak to one another, the less intimacy exists in the relationship. Talking to one another is important, but silence conveys a deeper expression of trust, commitment, and love.

Of course, this statement was met with great disbelief and incredulity among those so young for they had not yet had the opportunity to say "I love you" enough. But then neither

---

[11] The Word Among Us, August 2009, pg. 17.

had they felt the desperate need and intense release that comes when two souls become one spirit.

Spend twenty, thirty, forty, fifty years or a lifetime in love, and you will discover silence speaks louder than any words that could ever be spoken, and the greatest intimacy is achieved in the simple presence of another.

True intimacy engenders a close relationship, a sense of belonging and submission, a giving of one's self to someone without the expectation of anything in return. It is an aching awareness of, and an unquenchable longing for, the deepest knowing of another, a thing that can never be attained yet is forever sought.

Saint Augustine expressed his often distant and reluctant relationship with God this way:

> Late have I loved you,
> O Beauty ever ancient, ever new,
> late have I loved you!
> You were within me, but I was outside,
> and it was there that I searched for you.
>
> In my unloveliness
> I plunged into the lovely things which you created.
> You were with me, but I was not with you.
> Created things kept me from you;
> yet if they had not been in you
> they would have not been at all.

*You called, you shouted,*
*and you broke through my deafness.*
*You flashed, you shone,*
*and you dispelled my blindness.*

*You breathed your fragrance on me;*
*I drew in breath and now I pant for you.*
*I have tasted you,*
*now I hunger and thirst for more.*
*You touched me, and I burned for your peace.*[12]

Like Saint Augustine, we all too often find ourselves plunging into the lovely things which God has created, seeking intimacy in the external rather than within the silent sanctuary of our soul. Like moths to a flame, we are attracted to the bright lights and alluring sounds of the world: lovely things that are not God, that keep our eyes and ears, our hearts and minds turned away from Him.

Yet know that God awaits us in the intimacy of silence.

# The ambience of solitude

It is amazing how full our lives appear to be these days. With all of the labor-reducing, time-saving, energy-efficient, cost-effective devices at our disposal, you would think that we would have plenty of time to relax, read a book, watch a sunrise or a sunset, to think, to ponder or to pray. But do we?

---

[12] Saint Augustine, *Confessions*, Translated by Edward Bouverie Pusey, 401 A.D.

Jesus was a popular figure in his day; he was always engaged and in great demand. Traveling on foot from town to town preaching, often to large crowds numbering in the thousands, healing the sick, casting out demons, forgiving sins; he was a busy man. And yet he always found the time to be alone, to offer praise and prayer to his heavenly Father.

At the beginning of his public ministry, and after his baptism by John, he went off to the desert for forty days to fast and pray. *"Filled with the Holy Spirit, Jesus returned from the Jordan and was led by the Spirit into the desert for forty days, to be tempted by the devil."*[13]

Throughout his public life, he would seek out opportunities to be alone with God. *"Rising very early before dawn, he left and went off to a deserted place, where he prayed."*[14] *"And when he had taken leave of them, he went off to the mountain to pray."*[15] *"At daybreak, Jesus left and went to a deserted place."*[16] *"The report about him spread all the more, and great crowds assembled to listen to him and to be cured of their ailments, but he would withdraw to deserted places to pray."*[17] *"In those days he departed to the mountain to pray, and he spent the night in prayer to God."*[18]

---

[13] Lk 4:1-2
[14] Mk 1:35
[15] Mk 6:46
[16] Lk 4-42
[17] Lk 5:15
[18] Lk 6:12

At the end, on the evening before his death, he went off alone to pray. *"Then they came to a place named Gethsemane, and he said to his disciples, 'Sit here while I pray.' He took with him Peter, James, and John and began to be troubled and distressed... He advanced a little and fell to the ground and prayed..."*[19]

Jesus knew the absolute necessity for solitude, silence, and prayer. They are essential elements for living. Without solitude, without silence, without time spent in conversation with God, our lives can never be fully fed.

# The Serenity of Stillness

In Psalm 46, the LORD says, *"Be still and know that I am God."*[20] It is important to note that God doesn't tell us to *"be silent"* but quite emphatically commands us to *"be still"* and there is an enormous difference. '*Silence*' is defined as the forbearance from speech or noise, the absence of sound or noise while '*stillness*' is described as a state of tranquility or an instance of being quiet or calm, the absence of sound or noise, or the absence of motion or disturbance.

We can be silent in the midst of tumult and turmoil, but it is impossible for one to *"be still"* with a tormented mind, a tortured heart, or a disordered soul. What must be sought and attained is stillness within, an inward state of tranquility and peace that opens one's heart, mind, and soul to God. *"In our*

---

[19] Mk 14:32-33, 35
[20] Ps 46:11

stillness," E'yen A. Gardner writes, "*we acknowledge God's greatness and we are at peace in our life. Stillness saturates us in the Presence of God.*" He also points out that "*Being still does not mean don't move. It means move in peace.*"[21]

Aldous Huxley wrote, "*If a man would travel far along the mystic road, he must learn to desire God intensely but in stillness, passively and yet with all his heart and mind and strength.*"[22]

While we can earnestly search for and find solitude and silence, we may find that peace of mind, a quiet stillness from our thoughts and feelings to be elusive. To "*be still*" means we must empty ourselves, be at peace, and keep the world at bay. To "*be still*" requires that we empty our mind of all distracting thoughts while focusing only on conversing with God. We must rid our heart of all painful and negative thoughts, thoughts of anger, doubt, guilt, worry, frustration and fear, and fill our heart with love, hope, joy, peace, and compassion. We must cleanse our soul of all sin, corruption, and temptation so that we can create a spotless sanctuary for God.

There can be no question that stillness is far more difficult to achieve than either silence or solitude, for we have been conditioned to quite the opposite. In our overactive, multi-tasking, impatient, competitive world, stillness is to be avoided at all costs. For being still — what we often describe as doing

---

[21] E'yen A. Gardner, *Humbly Submitting to Change – The Wilderness Experience*, 2009

[22] Aldous Huxley, *The Perennial Philosophy*, 1945.

nothing — is considered wasting precious time. In our mind, we remember the old English proverb, *"An idle mind is the devil's workshop,"*[23] and so we crowd every second of our lives with busyness.

While stillness may be socially and culturally problematic, it is only because we have misconstrued its meaning and made it anathema within our daily lives. The reality is that we need a certain amount of stillness in much the same way as we need to close our eyes and sleep each day. To never 'be still' only serves to wear us out faster and sooner. But most importantly, it prevents us from having an intimate relationship with God.

To be silent, all one must do is close one's mouth and hold one's tongue. To find solitude, one must isolate one's self from all distractions and withdraw to a place of aloneness. But to *"be still,"* to find serenity and peace requires one to empty the mind, heart, and soul of all but God.

# Are you listening?

I have always been fascinated with books and the stories held within them. When I am reading I become immersed in the tale and the world that surrounds me disappears. All too often, my mother, a writer and a great lover of prose herself, would

---

[23] Anonymous, Old English proverb.

suddenly jar me away from my fantasy by saying, *"I know you can hear me, but you aren't listening."*

Jesus could have very well said those exact words to the Hebrews who heard him but refused to listen to what he had to say. When Jesus spoke, they often failed to listen. They spoke among themselves instead, questioning who he was and who he professed to be. To them, he was the son of the carpenter Joseph and his wife Mary, and he should know his place. Culturally it was unacceptable for him to be anything other than a carpenter just as his father, which only goes to show how little they really knew of him.

We all have a tendency to hear without listening. Our ears are constantly bombarded with sound and we have unconsciously learned to tune much of it out.

It is human nature to judge others based on our own experience, biases, and the immediacy of the moment. We hear, we decide, we judge, case closed. To listen so as to understand takes a certain amount of effort on our part, and within our busy lives, there is simply too little or no time.

How many of us have passed someone threadbare and unkempt on the street, and looked the other way or crossed the street to avoid being touched by someone less fortunate. Saint Paul tells us that *"The eye has not seen, and the ear has not heard, nor has it entered into the heart of man, what things God has prepared for those who love him."*[24]

If we are completely honest with ourselves, we would admit that we seldom, if ever, see or hear Jesus in a stranger. To someone we know well, we might say, *"she is an angel of God"* or *"he is such a kind, generous soul,"* but we never would speak of the stranger or the poor or the hungry in such a way. Rather, our thoughts turn to judgment, telling ourselves that it is their fault that they are who or what they are.

But Jesus made it abundantly clear that, unless we see him in everyone we meet and act accordingly, we will never be allowed to be in His presence. In the end, we will be judged on how well we fed the hungry and gave drink to the thirsty, welcomed the stranger and clothed the naked, cared for those who were ill and visited those who were in prison. As Jesus told us, *"Amen, I say to you, whatever you did for one of these least brothers of mine, you did for me."*[25]

We have eyes but do not see and ears but do not hear. We close our eyes and stopper our ears, but seldom do we shut our mouths. We surround ourselves with noise often of our own making to keep us from listening, from seeing, from feeling, from understanding. And as long as we continue to do so, we will never hear the voice of God, never feel His presence, and never see Jesus in the stranger.

---

[24] 1 Cor 2:9
[25] Mt 25:35-40

# To hear God you must listen

If you wish to hear God's voice, you must listen with all your heart, mind, and soul. This calls for us to take the first step in preparing ourselves to hear His voice by entering a place of silence, solitude, and stillness. For each of us, that place will be different and, at times, difficult to reach.

I was once asked how anyone could become still with all the distractions associated with daily living. It is seldom easy to be still, to find serenity amid chaos, peace surrounded by hatred, and tranquility within the bustle of our daily lives. To empty one's mind, heart, and soul of all but God seems like a pipe dream and an impossible quest. Yet it is not impossible. It is, in fact, entirely possible and absolutely essential although it may initially take a fair amount of effort to achieve.

You might begin by finding a place of quiet solitude where you are alone. This might be a seat in your garden, a room in your home, or a pew in the church. Close your eyes and relax. Try to let go of any conscious thoughts. Pray the rosary. Reflect on the mysteries as you pray, and you will soon discover that all other thoughts have been pushed into a corner of your mind allowing your thoughts to be with God. When you find your mind wandering, focus on the words you are praying. Let them become a mantra that dispels all unwanted worldly distractions.

Once you are still, in a solitary place, and silent, you are then ready to take the second step, which is to listen for God's voice.

Listening is an important life skill. We listen to learn, to understand, to be informed, and even for pleasure. We listen not only with our ears but with all of our senses as well as with our eyes and our intuition.

You might think that with all the listening we do that we are naturally good listeners, but sadly, it just isn't so. Studies suggest that we remember less than half of what we hear. Think about it. In any ten-minute conversation, perhaps as few as two minutes, and at most five minutes of it, will be remembered.

To really listen, you must pay careful attention to what is being said. You must actively listen while making a conscious effort not only to hear what is being said, but to try to understand what you are hearing. Too often we find ourselves waiting for our chance to speak and to be heard.

If you are distracted, you aren't really listening. If you are thinking of how to respond to whatever is being discussed, you aren't really listening. If you are bored or thinking of other things, you aren't really listening. If you aren't listening then you aren't hearing and cannot fully understand what is being said.

It is no small wonder that we seldom, if ever, hear God for we are such poor listeners. God rarely speaks to us in normal conversation. As with Elijah, God was not in the strong and heavy wind nor the earthquake nor the fire; rather, God was in the tiny whispering sound. To hear God, we must listen in silence and solitude with a stillness of heart, mind and soul.

# Chapter Two

## Lord, teach us to pray

*He was praying in a certain place,*
*and when he had finished,*
*one of his disciples said to him,*
*"Lord, teach us to pray*
*just as John taught his disciples."*

*He said to them, "When you pray, say:*

*Father, hallowed be your name,*
*your kingdom come.*
*Give us each day our daily bread*
*and forgive us our sins*
*for we ourselves forgive everyone*
*in debt to us,*
*and do not subject us*
*to the final test."*

Luke 11:1-4

# Taking God for granted

Do you pray? If you were asked this question, how would you respond? I often ask this question of the young adults that I teach. Unfortunately, all too often the answer is a resounding "No!" We find ourselves too busy, too distracted, or too involved in the world around us to pray.

But what if you woke up tomorrow and all you had was what you thanked God for today?

I have to admit that when I first read that question, it made me feel quite uncomfortable. I had to stop and ask myself if I had given Him even a small portion of praise and thanksgiving for all that I had received. Upon reflection, I realized that I have too often fallen short in giving Him thanks. I discovered that far too often, if I answered the question honestly, I would wake up tomorrow with very little indeed.

Everything that I have, everything that I am, all that I will ever be are gifts from God; gifts that He has freely given, no strings attached. All too often I simply take it all for granted without any consideration for, or acknowledgement of, the one who has given it all to me. And so the question causes me to pause and really consider how I ought to respond.

How often do we focus on all that has gone wrong with our day: the injustices we have incurred, the injuries we have sustained, the problems we have faced? We complain and heap pity on ourselves for having lived through such a thoroughly rotten day and we look up to heaven and cry, "*Why me, God? What did I do to deserve all this?*"

If we are honest with ourselves, I would suspect that most of us can recall how, on more than one occasion, we have asked God, "*Why me?*" But I wonder how many of us can recall thanking Him for all of the good things that have come our way, and the wonderful gifts we have received from Him. I suspect that, should we tally the "*why me's*" and the "*thank you's,*" the former would far outweigh the latter by a very wide margin.

There is a scene from the movie BRUCE ALMIGHTY where Bruce (who has been given all the powers of God) is sitting in front of his computer receiving messages from all of humanity, and he is quickly overwhelmed with all of the whining and begging — all the "*why me's.*" If only He could have received a simple "*thank you.*"

So for tomorrow, and all of the tomorrows yet to come, let us take a moment to remember to thank God for the gifts we received today. I am sure He would appreciate the gratitude. And who knows, you might wake up tomorrow with more than you had today!

# A surge of the heart

What is prayer and how should we pray? These are questions that have been voiced many times, even by the apostles. Jesus gave us the Lord's Prayer, that perfect plea which contains all that we rightly desire before God.

Saint John Damascene wrote that *"Prayer is the raising of one's mind and heart to God or the requesting of good things from God."*[26] Saint Therese of Lisieux wrote that *"For me, prayer is a surge of the heart; it is a simple look turned toward heaven, it is a cry of recognition and of love, embracing both trial and joy."*[27]

> *I used to never pray, Lord.*
> *You would never see me on my knees.*
> *And now*
> *You bent my knees Lord, You hit me hard.*
> *O Lord,*
> *I pray that what I pray will be enough.*[28]

When we pray, we must do so with great humility and contrition. Jesus illustrated this through the parable of the Pharisee and the Tax Collector. He tells us that *"... for everyone who exalts himself will be humbled, and the one who humbles himself will be exalted."*[29] Humility is the foundation of prayer.

Just as Jesus tells us how to pray, he also admonishes us that *"when you pray, do not be like the hypocrites, who love to stand*

---

[26] Catechism of the Catholic Church, no. 2559.

[27] Ibid, no. 2558.

[28] C. R. Lanham, A *Poem for the Day: June 8, 2009.*

[29] Lk 18:9-14

*and pray in the synagogues and on street corners so that others may see them. Amen, I say to you, they have received their reward. But when you pray, go to your inner room, close the door, and pray to your Father in secret. And your Father who sees in secret will repay you."*[30]

Within each of us, there is a singular and solitary place for God. It is our soul, a sanctuary where a covenantal relationship exists between one's self and God. It is a place for reflection and conversation, joy and sorrow, honesty and trust. It is where prayer is made and prayer is answered.

In teaching us how to pray, Jesus tells us that *"Your Father knows what you need before you ask him."*[31] God knows what you truly need rather than what you think you need. And that is why we often believe that our prayers go unanswered. We pray and pray, fervently asking God to help us, give us, cure us, free us, or save us. When our pleas go unanswered, we shake our heads in frustration and blame Him for our misery and for our failures.

But did God ignore our prayer or did we ignore his response? God knows what you need even when you do not. It is our failure to understand the purpose and power of prayer that gets in the way. It is our misconception of our relationship with God that turns our prayer inside out. God is our creator and it is He who is in control. We owe our existence to the One who made us. He owes us nothing. We owe Him everything.

---

[30] Mt 6:5-6
[31] Mt 6:8

Our prayers to God should not be pleas of supplication but rather *"a cry of recognition and of love, embracing both trial and joy."*[32]

God always responds, but He responds to us in His own time and in His own way. As long as we look toward Him for the answers that we expect when we expect them, we will miss the response that He will provide. Praise God, thank God, love God and He will reward you with all that you need: the gifts of His grace and love.

## Perfect prayer

In the Gospel of Luke,[33] Jesus responds to his disciples' request to teach them how to pray. Luke writes a much abbreviated version from that of Matthew,[34] which is nearest in form to that which we are most familiar. While there should be little doubt that the beatitudes are prayer, the Lord's Prayer is quite unique in its form and substance as a true and perfect offering of prayer to God our Father. While Jesus often went away to be alone and pray, we know little or nothing of what he prayed. The Lord's Prayer is the only prayer that Jesus gave us and it is, indeed, a perfect one.

Saint Thomas Aquinas wrote that *"The Lord's Prayer is the most perfect of prayers... In it we ask, not only for all the things we*

---

[32] Saint Therese of Lisieux, *Manuscrits autobiographiques.*
[33] Lk 11:2-4
[34] Mt 6:9-13

*can rightly desire, but also in the sequence that they should be desired. This prayer not only teaches us to ask for things, but also in what order we should desire them.*"[35]

The Lord's Prayer is perhaps the most recited prayer for all Christians. As Catholics, we pray it within every Mass, multiple times when we pray the rosary, and on many other occasions. We know it so thoroughly that through countless repetition, we mindlessly repeat its words with little or no thought to what we are saying. And when we finish, we seldom give a moment's consideration to what we have just prayed.

The Lord's Prayer is the perfect communal prayer. It is not and never has been a private or a personal prayer, but rather a prayer professed together in communion with our brothers and sisters. Say or read the prayer and you will discover that there are no singular pronouns to be found. No "*I*," no "*me*," no "*my*," no "*mine*," only "*our*," "*us*," and "*we*." When we pray "*Our Father…*" we are praying in unity with our brothers and sisters, all created by God in His image and likeness. We do not pray alone but united as one body, one creation of God, for God, to God.

Saint John Chrysostom tells us that "[*The Lord*] *teaches us to make prayer in common for all our brethren. For he did not say*

---

[35] Saint Thomas Aquinas, *Summa Theologica*, II, II, 83.

'My' Father who are in heaven, but 'Our' Father, offering petitions for the common body."[36]

Jesus taught us that the greatest commandment is to love God with all our heart, with all our mind, and with all our soul. He added emphatically *"love your neighbor as yourself."* The measure with which we love one another, and the extent to which we can forgive one another, are perfect indicators of the measure and extent to which we love God. We can only ask God to forgive us to the extent that we forgive others. Without forgiveness toward others, we cannot ask God to forgive us. After all, it is what we say when we pray to our Father isn't it?

# A prayer of gratitude

I suspect that many of us can remember being taught by our parents and teachers how to recite our prayers, and to say them on our knees before we went to bed each night. We were probably taught to ask God to help us with all the important issues that confronted us in our daily lives. We looked to God as the purveyor of goodness and the giver of all that we believed we needed: *"God, I really need to pass the exam tomorrow. God, help me find a job. God, I really need to win the lottery."*

The fact is that for most of us, prayer is a one-way conversation. We talk but never listen. It is no small wonder that the most common complaint heard is *"I pray and pray and*

---

[36] Saint John Chrysostom, *Homilies on the Gospel of St. Matthew.*

*pray but God never answers.*" If all we do is talk, how can we possibly hear what God might have to say?

Imagine sitting down with a friend whom you have known for a very long time. Your friend begins the conversation and then continues to talk, and talk, and talk, and talk and …. You are never given the opportunity to speak. Good conversation requires active participation from all parties, both talking and listening. Why shouldn't the same hold true in prayer with God?

*"But I listen but God never speaks."* Really? I suppose that if you are expecting a deep booming voice speaking from the clouds, you may be correct. God only responds that way in the movies. God responds to us in many ways, but we have to be open to His Voices. Look around you. Open your heart and mind. Empty yourself of all but God so that you may hear God.

When all we do is ask God for what we think we need or want, we are really separating ourselves from Him. It is as though we believe that God has no clue as to what is going on in our lives so we feel the need to explicitly inform Him. God knows what we need. He always has and always will. There is no need to bring Him up to date. Looking at it that way, the *"I need"* now becomes *"because you are aware"* or *"since you know where I am right now."*

The most common excuse that I hear for not praying is that there simply is not enough time to pray. Is that right? Just how long does it take to offer a prayer to God? Consider how long it would take to offer this prayer to God; it only requires two words: *"Thank You."*

Meister Eckhart believed that this was more than sufficient. He wrote, *"If the only prayer you say in your whole life is 'Thank You,' that would suffice."*[37] All you have to do is thank God and then be still and listen. God loves you, knows what you need, and always appreciates your gratitude.

For contemplatives, one word is better than two words in prayer. The anonymous author of The Cloud of Unknowing writes *"Contemplatives seldom use words when they pray, but if they do, they choose only a few, and the fewer the better. They prefer a short one-syllable word over two syllables, because the spirit can best assimilate it."*[38] The author urges those who would pray to empty their minds of every thought but God, and to fill themselves with God. The author offers a telling example of the efficacy of short prayer:

> *When a person is terrified by a fiery catastrophe, someone's death, or something similar, they cry out for help. That's obvious. But what do they say? I can promise you a person in danger won't pray a long string of words or even a word of two syllables. Why not? When desperate, you've got no time to waste. At your wits' end and scared to death, there's no time for*

---

[37] Matthew Fox, Meditations with Meister Eckhart, pg. 34, 1983.
[38] Carmen Acevedo Butcher, *Anonymous, The Cloud of Unknowing: A New Translation,* 2011.

*babbling or big words — you'll scream, 'Fire!' or 'Help!'
and this one-word outburst works best.*[39]

Now I cannot accurately measure how long a one or two word prayer would take to utter, but it would appear to be somewhere approaching *'no time at all'* and the best part is that you are not required to pray it out loud. In fact, it is suggested that you pray this prayer in silence. Thus you are no longer relegated to any specific time or place for you to pray. Do you have any other excuse?

# Every soul is a song

Every soul is a song, an anthem to the wonder and majesty of God, an infinite melody in prayer to the One who caused us all to become. When it comes to communicating with Almighty God, we often develop a severe case of something akin to stage fright, stuttering and stammering and suddenly finding ourselves incapable of expressing the simplest coherent thought.

We are beggars seeking His grace, forgiveness, love, mercy, embrace, help, guidance, or any number of untold favors or requests, and our unworthiness keeps us at a distance from Him. But as someone once said, *"God understands our prayers even when we cannot find the words to say them."*[40]

---

[39] Ibid.
[40] Unknown.

Few would consider prayer a natural act, a thing innate within our hearts, for we bear that human conceit which believes that we are in control. And it is inevitable that, in that moment when we encounter our unworthiness, when we are confronted with our own frailties and sinfulness, that in helpless desolation, we seek the divine.

Small wonder we bend a knee, mouth agape, wondering how to approach God without groveling. Ernesto Cardenal, a Nicaraguan priest, wrote that *"Prayer is as natural to man as speaking, sighing and seeing, as natural as the palpitation of a loving heart; and actually that is what prayer is: a murmur, a sigh, a glance, a heartbeat of love."*[41] God loves us and tells us that any expression of love is a prayer. He even admonishes us to *"love your neighbor as yourself."*[42]

Yet we continue to struggle in our communication with God. God is too big, too much. It is too difficult to pray, too difficult to find the words, too overwhelming to express ourselves to the Unknowable. But perhaps we are merely trying too hard.

Again, Ernesto Cardenal tells us, *"Prayer is nothing more than getting into intimate contact with God. It is communication with God, and as such it need not be expressed in words, nor even articulated mentally. One can communicate with a glance of the eyes,*

---

[41] Ernesto Cardenal, *To Live Is to Love: Meditations on Love and Spirituality,* 1974.
[42] Lev 19:18.

*with a smile, with a sigh, as well as by a human act. Even ... the painting of a picture, or a look toward heaven or the taking of a drink of water [can be a prayer]."*[43]

Matthew Fox further expresses this sentiment by writing, *"Our actions can be prayers. Indeed, they ought to be if they come truly and spontaneously from our heart, which is also where our authentic work and actions derive from. Drinking water – if done with gratitude and awareness – is a prayer. So is painting a picture or study or dance – if it truly comes from a deep, heart place."*[44]

Every act, every breath, every thought can be and ought to be prayer, for we have been created out of Love, by Love, for Love, to love. God created us to love and to be loved, and it is our love of life – all life – which is the most perfect form of prayer. Simply put, if we love, when we love, as we love, we are in prayer for our very existence is a form of prayer; there is no escape. We may ignore it, but we cannot avoid it.

So waking in gratitude, breathing in life, dancing in love, weeping in sorrow, embracing the day: let us pray, let us pray.

---

[43] Ernesto Cardenal, *To Live Is to Love: Meditations on Love and Spirituality*, 1974.

[44] Matthew Fox, Christian Mystics: 365 Readings and Meditations, pg 345, 2011.

# Chapter Three

## If today you hear his voice

Enter, let us bow down in worship;
let us kneel before the LORD who made us.
For this is our God,
whose people we are,
God's well-tended flock.

Oh, that today you would hear his voice:
Do not harden your hearts …

Psalm 95:6-8

We all have questions concerning God. We wonder sometimes if He even exists because He never seems to speak to us. He never responds to our pleas and our prayers. No one has ever seen God and most would state quite emphatically that they have never heard His voice. But is that true?

## God never shouts

In the beginning God created man and woman, and since they were all alone, God kept company with them and spoke with them directly and often. After all, they had been created by Him in His image and they had many questions to ask of their creator. There were no televisions, radios, iPods, cellphones, or computers to occupy their time or overload their senses. The quiet solitude of the garden provided the perfect setting for having casual and intimate conversations between themselves and their creator; nothing to interrupt or distract them from their close relationship with God.

God is present everywhere and every time. He is integral and inseparable to all that is, was, and ever shall be. To hear God's voice, all we have to do is listen. But be aware that God never raises His voice. He never shouts. He speaks softly, and you must listen with a quiescent mind and an attentive ear to hear His voice.

When God created man and woman, He gave each a voice. When they were only two, they could easily speak and be heard by one another. But as humanity grew, so did the voices.

And unlike God, we all too often raise our voices shouting over one another to be heard. God's voice has been lost in the cacophony of sound that we produce. The din has become so deafening that we can seldom hear ourselves think, let alone hear God.

In ancient times, the noise was far less than it is today. Throughout the Old Testament, we read of God speaking to those who remained steadfast in their faith and belief in Him. Often God spoke through messengers because the increasing clamor and noise drowned out or suppressed the hearing of His Word. His messengers often had to shout to be heard, and were ignored or punished for speaking in His name.

God speaks to us as much today as He did in the beginning. He has never turned His back on us nor has He left us alone. Each of us, at some moment in our life, has voiced the complaint that God has failed to respond to our prayers. We pray and beseech Him to relieve our suffering, cure our ills, wash away our sins, and forgive us for all our transgressions. For all our prayers, we hear nothing in return. We feel abandoned and ignored by God.

Our failure to hear God's response is not the result of Him ignoring our plea but a failure on our part to listen in the quiet stillness of His presence. God never shouts. If we refuse to cancel out the noise that surrounds us, then we will never hear His response.

Remove the distractions. Turn off the technology. Turn down the blinding, glaring lights. Enter into the serenity that was present in the garden created in the beginning where you can be alone with your God.

Listen in silence. Listen in solitude. Listen in stillness. Listen, really listen, and you will hear the voice of God.

## We are filled with God

Julian of Norwich, a fourteenth century Benedictine nun and mystic, beautifully describes God's presence this way: "*We are in God and God whom we do not see is in us.*"[45]

Another point of view, one that is all too commonly held, is that God is out there someplace. Consider that we almost universally look up toward heaven to find Him and down to, well...you know where, for you know who.

We read, "*God said: 'Let us make man in our image, after our likeness' ... God created man in his image, in the divine image He created him, male and female He created them*"[46] and, without hesitation and with great hubris, we blithely reverse the process and create God in our own image. If this appears to be excessively overstating the case, consider the **Creation of Adam that** marvelous fresco painted on the ceiling of the Sistine Chapel by Michelangelo.

---

[45] Brendan Doyle, *Meditations with Julian of Norwich*, 1983.
[46] Gn 1:26-27

Isaiah recounts to us that *"the virgin shall be with child, and bear a son, and shall name him Immanuel."*[47] Prophetically speaking, *'Immanuel'* in Hebrew עִמָּנוּאֵל means *'God is with us.'* It would appear that even from the earliest of times wildly opposing views on the nature of God and His presence among us have occupied our thoughts and intrigued us to no end. But then for much of human history, the universe revolved around the earth and the earth itself was flat. To borrow a phrase from a popular commercial, *"everybody knows that."*

Given that we have so indelicately put God in His place *up there* and molded Him to perfectly fit into our own self-image, it is completely baffling to many as to why we cannot carry on a decent conversation with Him whom we have so carefully constructed. After all, He has a mouth just as we do, so why doesn't He open His and speak to us? It is most certainly a conundrum of the highest order.

Despite what we might believe or wish to believe, we did not create God in our own image. Sorry to disappoint you. God created us, and as Jesus promised, *"behold, I am with you always, until the end of the age,"*[48] words that tell us that His real, yet invisible, presence will always be with us echoing the prophesy of Isaiah that *'God is with us.'*

We are filled with God. Every molecule and atom of our being, and even the insubstantial essence of our soul, contains

---

[47] Is 7:14
[48] Mt 28:42

His love and divinity. We can no more eliminate God from our lives than we can dissolve or wish our own self into non-existence. As long as we are and will be – and our soul will exist for all eternity – we are intimately bound by His divine gravity from which there is no escape velocity.

When we consider how closely we are intertwined with God, is it any wonder that we cannot hear Him speak to us? After all, when have you ever heard a single cell of yours speak to you?

Julian of Norwich also said, *"God is everything that is good and the goodness that everything possesses is God."*[49] God is all that is good for God is good, and because God is all good, all good that we come to experience must be from God.

## God is always near

Many times we wonder whether God is listening because He seems so far way, so remote. At times we may even feel as though God has left us completely to our own devices, and abandoned us for a more obeisant and believing crowd. Our doubts and feelings of abandonment cause us to ask the question: If God is omnipresent, why is His silence so deafening, His love so remote?

There is a certain rhythm and flow to every life unique unto itself; every measured beat differs from the one that came

---

[49] Brendan Doyle, *Meditations with Julian of Norwich*, 1983.

before and only God can play its melody. It is our own arrogance and conceit that fills us with everything but God, and propels us to create God in our own image. We cry out in wonder and mystery that God has forsaken us, abandoned us when we need Him most. But has He?

The fourteenth century mystic Meister Eckhart tells us that *"God is in the soul with His nature, with His being, and with His Godhead, and yet God is not the soul."*[50] Your soul is yours alone, created by God and forever filled with God, but never God. God never leaves us, but we often leave God.

Henry David Thoreau wrote, *"Most men lead lives of quiet desperation and go to the grave with the song still in them."*[51] We live our lives desperately searching for the false gods of fame and fortune. We fill ourselves with the world and all its seductive yet empty promises in a vain attempt to find God within ourselves, and always we come away empty, wanting more and more, always more. We never recognize that we are God's song, a song too often left unsung.

Meister Eckhart wrote that *"I pray God to rid me of God"*[52] by which he prays for God's forgiveness and help in ridding himself of his own self-centered perceptions and his flawed human image of God. We all have a personal image of God and we all too readily try to conform that image to our own when

---

[50] Raymond B. Blakney, *Meister Eckhart: A Modern Translation*, 1941.
[51] Henry David Thoreau, *Civil Disobedience*, 1849.
[52] Matthew Fox, *Passion for Creation: The Earth-Honoring Spirituality of Meister Eckhart*, 2000.

even a cursory review of the first page of the Bible would quickly dismiss that notion. *"Then God said: 'Let us make man in our image, after our likeness,'"*[53] and a short verse later, *"God created man in his image, in the divine image He created him; male and female He created them."*[54]

When we fill ourselves with everything but God, we empty ourselves of God. Darkness envelops us and hides all our imperfections; it hides the truth that lives only in the light. We bury the light that is the inner beauty, truth, and goodness of God with created things that are not God.

We each have had moments when our faith and devotion to God were less than they ought to be: moments spent in anger, doubt, frustration, anxiety, fear, arrogance or pride. It is tempting to live in darkness away from the transparency that comes when we expose the interior to the light. To live in the light means to live openly, honestly, and transparently, with nothing hidden, with no deception or guile.

Saint John Chrysostom believed that the light *"illuminates also the beholder's mind and soul. It disperses the darkness of evil, and invites those who encounter it to let their own light shine forth, and to follow the example of virtue.... Let your virtue, the perfection of your life, and the performance of good works inspire those who see you to*

---

[53] Gn 1:26
[54] Gn 1:27

*praise the common Master of us all. And so I beg each of you to strive to live so perfectly that the LORD may be praised by all who see you."*[55]

# Does God have a voice, can He speak?

Father John Foley once penned, *"We are God's song....Let your life sing, let it sing. Let your life be what it is: God's joyous, interleaved and always consonant melody, sounding outwards in deepest joy."*[56]

Imagine! We are God's song! Sing a song of joy and exultation to the life that we are given by God for in a very profound way God sings each of us into existence giving voice to our unique and marvelous music. Zephaniah tells us that the LORD *"will sing joyfully because of you, as one sings at festivals."*[57]

Those who came to John the Baptist asked him, *"What then should we do?"*[58] and were told to sing praise and glorify the LORD through their lives. Share with others who are less fortunate, treat everyone with fairness and kindness, live in truth and love for those around you, lose yourself in humility and truth and, above all, trust and love the LORD.

---

[55] Saint John Chrysostom, *Eighth Baptism Catecheses*, c. 347-407.
[56] John Foley, SJ, *Advent Song, Spirituality of the Readings*, Dec 16, 2012, http://liturgy.slu.edu/3AdvC121612/reflections_foley.html.
[57] Zep 3:18
[58] Lk 3:10

Saint Paul tells us to *"Rejoice in the LORD always....Your kindness should be known to all. The LORD is near."*[59] Jesus is near. He is always close, watching and waiting for those moments when we are weak or failing, ready to lift us up and give us the grace and strength to sing a song of thanksgiving to God.

The *Good News* is that we are never alone, for He is always near. Look around and you will see Him. Open your hearts and you will feel Him. Sit quietly and you will hear Him. Stand silently and you will feel His warm embrace.

God's song is eternal and everywhere. You can neither silence it nor can you stop it from playing. It is a wondrous melody full of life and living sung with unceasing and unbounded love and loving.

*"And the Word became flesh and made his dwelling among us, and we saw his glory, the glory as of the Father's only Son, full of grace and truth."*[60] The Word became man, Jesus Christ, the Son of God, to bring light to the world, *"[w]hat came to be through him was life, and this life was the light of the human race; the light shines in the darkness, and the darkness has not overcome it."*[61]

His was the voice of God made flesh. He came to redeem us from our sins and He is with us always. He is a song of ecstasy and agony, of hope and salvation, death and resurrection, peace and love.

---

[59] Phil 4:4-5
[60] Jn 1:14
[61] Jn 1:3b-5

We are the body of Christ. We are God's song. At his birth, the heavenly hosts sang a song of peace and goodwill toward all. So it is perfectly apropos for us to lift up our voices in song to God. Let us sing our song of joy to God.

# God is calling

*"Oh, that today you hear His voice, do not harden your hearts."*[62] Psalm 95 calls us to open our hearts and to listen with a willing and honest ear to hear God's voice. How often do you hear God's voice? If we listen – really listen – we will hear God speak to us every day in a myriad of ways, through many different voices.

Seldom does He speak in that deep theatrical voice we are presented with in film and theater. He certainly has never spoken to me that way. It would be interesting if He did, but I won't hold my breath. More often than not, God speaks with a voice that is difficult to hear above the clamor and noise that surrounds us. His voice is often just *"a tiny whispering sound"*[63] that requires our devoted attention to hear it.

We are so tuned into all the noise that emanates from the plethora of technological gadgetry available to us, that it is small wonder we seldom find a moment's peace. Silence and solitude are becoming increasingly rare commodities, and the

---

[62] Ps 95:7-8
[63] 1 Kgs 19:12

noise has become so loud and pervasive that one cannot begin to think!

But no matter how loud or distracting the noise, the reality is that God is constantly speaking to us. It is like the philosophical question: *"If a tree falls in a forest and no one is around to hear it, does it make a sound?"*[64] It is a question concerning reality and our perception of it.

Rene Descartes proposed a bit of casuistry by stating, *"Cogito ergo sum – I think, therefore I am"*[65] and, unfortunately, far too many have blithely accepted Descartes' proposition as truth. What is true is that Descartes got it backwards, for one cannot think one's self into existence. It would have been far more accurate to have said, *"I am, therefore I think."* To think presupposes the reality of one's prior creation and existence. To think means to use one's mind, to search for understanding, to seek the truth. To think requires a willingness to listen with silent stillness to hear the voice of God.

God indeed exists and He speaks to each of us every day. He speaks to us in so many ways. All we have to do is (to paraphrase Timothy Leary) *"turn off, tune in, and listen up."* We may never know when or in what voice God will speak to us. We may hear His voice anytime and anywhere. It may be a message on a billboard as you pass it by, or it may be a word or a sentence that you read in a book, magazine, or newspaper.

---

[64] Unknown.
[65] Rene Descartes, *Discourse on the Method*, 1637.

You may see it painted on the sky at sunrise or sunset or upon the tranquil waters of an ocean or a lake. You may hear God speak through a stranger, a chance encounter, a conversation overheard, or a discussion over dinner with family and friends.

The truth is that God is seldom silent while we seldom listen. What is true is that God is always calling, so why not answer His call?

## If you hear God's voice

Have you ever considered how many times the LORD speaks to someone in the Bible? It is a rare week that we fail to hear of the LORD – whether to Elijah or Abraham, Moses or Daniel – giving voice and direction to someone. God's voice is seldom if ever described beyond the words that were heard.

A song written by David Haas contains the refrain, *"If today you hear God's voice, harden not your heart."*[66] This refrain is, of course, taken from Psalm 95, which is both a song of acclamation to the power of God and a poem of prophetic rebuke to the wayward people of Israel. It comes at a pivotal point that marks both the ending of the acclamation and the beginning of the rebuke.

What is perhaps of utmost importance for us today is what is implied, rather than explicitly stated, within this poetic

---

[66] David Haas, *Glory to God: The Best of David Haas, Vol. 4, If Today You Hear God's Voice*, Jul 1, 2009.

verse. What is assumed in this statement is that, if you can hear God's voice then, God must *have* a voice that speaks in a way you are capable of hearing and understanding.

The question is: how will I know when God is speaking to me? After all, God doesn't have a daily radio or television show where you can tune in to hear His Word. So how are we to know when God has something to tell us?

A few years ago, I enjoyed watching JOAN OF ARCADIA, an Emmy award-winning television show that told the story of teenager Joan Girardi, who each week encountered and spoke with God and performed some task that she was given. Each week God appeared to Joan as an ordinary human being, and each week He was a different person. One week God was a little girl, then a dog walker, next week a trash man, then a newscaster, a housewife, hall monitor, groundskeeper, or a street guitarist.

Reflecting on how God spoke with Joan, I realized that this might be one of the many possible ways that God might speak to each of us. When you consider that God is with us and in us, always and everywhere, why should He not speak to us through one another? We are called to see Christ, the Son of God, in every face we meet. If so, then what does that tell us about where we might hear His voice?

Once, not long ago, I spent an evening with a cousin whose husband was nearing the end of his life. I arrived at their home filled with questions, wondering why him, why now? He was several years younger than I, at that point in life where he was perhaps best able to enjoy his children and grandchildren, family and friends. He had a brilliant mind and I felt he had yet so much to offer. It felt as though the loss from his absence would simply be too great when compared to what he might yet have to give.

I quickly came to realize that God was with us that evening in a very real sense, and that He had answered all my questions, every last one of them. I heard God in the voices of my cousin and her husband. I saw Him through the eyes and voice of someone who was ready to meet and speak directly with God – no more middleman – and I knew that I would continue to hear his voice in my heart and in my soul.

God does speak to each of us. He answers all our prayers and gives us all that we need to live our lives as He intends. To hear His voice you must look for Him, see Him in others, and then listen with an open heart and mind. I can't promise that He will tell you what you expect or want to hear but then what can you do? After all, He IS God.

# Chapter Four

## A tiny whispering sound

At the mountain of God, Horeb,
Elijah came to a cave where he took shelter.
Then the LORD said to him, "Go outside and stand
on the mountain before the LORD;
the LORD will be passing by."

A strong and heavy wind was rending
the mountains and crushing rocks before the LORD —
but the LORD was not in the wind.
After the wind there was an earthquake—
but the LORD was not in the earthquake.
After the earthquake there was fire—
but the LORD was not in the fire.

After the fire there was a tiny whispering sound.

When he heard this, Elijah hid his face in his cloak
and went and stood at the entrance of the cave.

1 Kings 19:9a, 11-13a

# A tiny whispering sound

One thing I have discovered is that God never feels the need to rush into things. After all, He is beyond time and place; what will happen is happening and has happened. I have also come to believe that He has a marvelous sense of humor, and derives no small amount of enjoyment in observing our feeble attempts to do things on our own without His love and support.

For more than thirty years, I refused to have any connection with God, and for the most part, He patiently obliged. Like a petulant child who stubbornly ignores whoever happens to be the offender of some perceived injustice, I saw no need to engage with Him in dialog or even to acknowledge my dependence on Him. Oh, I recognized that He was there and never doubted His presence. I simply found it easier to ignore Him and to do as I pleased, without concerning myself with how He might react or what He might think.

But God never leaves us to our own devices no matter how much we might try to push Him away. He reacts to our rejection much like "no-see-ums" on a sweltering summer's day; nearly invisible and highly annoying, you cannot resist them, harm them, or catch them and, perhaps most irritating of all, you simply cannot ignore them. In general, you are reduced to swatting helplessly at them and dashing for some form of cover to elude their insistent distraction.

For the longest time, I pushed God from my mind and heart. I had more important matters to consider: family, friends, business, living the good life and enjoying all its pleasures. I simply had no time left for Him. Externally, life was good, full of sunshine and laughter, great success and reward while internally the light within my soul was gradually dimming, slowly but inexorably fading into darkness.

Like an addict, each success and every achievement became less satisfying than the one before. Good feelings – joy, peace, love, contentment, happiness – were over time replaced with increased feelings of emptiness, anger, dissatisfaction, rage, resentment, hatred, and unhappiness. I was never satisfied. I continually needed more: more money, more power, more prestige, more, more, always more. I failed to realize it at the time, but I was feeding my body while starving my soul.

Sadly, I believe there are far too many of us who find ourselves gorging at the banquet of life while totally ignoring food for the soul; suffering simultaneously from secular gluttony and spiritual anorexia.

Looking back, I realize that while I was chasing success and ignoring my soul, God was constantly nagging my conscience like a swarm of no-see-ums, reminding me that I was slowly starving to death. He was not going to let go or surrender me to the black hole of emptiness and death.

While I refused to listen to what He was saying, He made sure I knew He was there. Small insistent voices, silent yet often so loud they hurt, would speak to me telling me to turn away from the darkness and open myself to His light. As quickly as they were born, I silenced them, refusing to allow them to break free and grow. But God is persistent and He kept at it for over thirty years. As hard as I tried, I could neither find cover nor silence the voices.

I seldom bent my knee in prayer for, in truth, I had no authentic understanding of it. I grew up the oldest of eleven in a devout Catholic family. I attended twelve years of Catholic school taught by Dominican sisters who wore full body armor (habits.) I attended Mass every Sunday along with my parents, was an altar server, and sang in the choir. I could recite all the standard prayers – the Lord's Prayer, Hail Mary, Glory Be, etc. – but was never taught how to pray. I must confess that I never really bothered to learn how to pray or investigate what it truly meant to be in communion with God.

It simply never occurred to me that prayer was meant to be bi-directional, or that I was supposed to occasionally shut up and listen. And I am quite certain that, had I listened, I would have never heard God's voice for I never bothered to tune my heart to His voice. I was, as the song goes, *"looking for love in all the wrong places,"*[67] and never bothered to turn on the receiver.

In order to hear God, one must tune into Him with a humble heart, an open mind, and a receptive soul. You must

---

[67] Wanda Mallette, Bob Morrison, and Patti Ryan, *Lookin' for Love*, recorded by Johnny Lee, June 1980.

turn up your sacred hearing aid and listen. Listen with quiet earnestness and you will hear a tiny whispering sound, and the LORD will be in that tiny whispering sound.

Throughout the thirty years that I was wandering lost in the desert of my life, I heard many tiny whispering sounds, but never took the time nor made any attempt to listen or to hear their music. They were simply annoying persistent nags on my conscience; tiny whispering sounds that cried *"You need Me"* and *"I am here."*

I heard God's voice at the most inopportune times, those moments of weakened conscience and raw emotion. Surprisingly, I would hear His voice most often when mine was raised in anger and frustration. No matter how loud my voice became, it could never silence or overwhelm His. It was at those moments that I heard His voice above all others. My mind and heart would suddenly be tuned to His frequency and all other voices, including my own, would be cancelled out. But hearing is not the same as listening, and although I heard His voice, I was neither willing nor prepared to listen; listening to God remained a long time off. Thank God, for He is eternally patient.

## Indistinctly, as in a mirror

When you ask God for help, it is important to be prepared to recognize His response in the unexpected and the ordinary; for the reality is that God seldom responds in an expected or spectacular way. There is a parable that illustrates how God often responds to our pleas, and how we should be open to His response no matter how unexpected.

There was once a woman, a widow advanced in age, who had lived for many years in a small house located near the banks of a mighty river. She spent much of her days in prayer, attended Mass each day, and prayed the Rosary on her knees each evening before retiring for the night. Each morning she would rise and bend her knees in prayer and thanksgiving to God for giving her another day.

In the early spring, the rains came even as the snow melted in lands far to the north, and overnight the river overcame its banks and flooded the land where her home was located. When the waters reached her knees, she looked to heaven with calm assurance that God would save her from any harm. As she stood there with the water swirling around her, a boat floated nearby and the occupants offered to take her to safety. The woman thanked them, but declined their offer with firm resolve, stating that God would save her.

As the water continued to rise, the woman was forced to take refuge on the roof of her home. Not long after, another boat drifted by and again she was offered a place in the boat, and again she declined with confidence that God would soon save her.

After some more time had passed, while she stood at the highest point of the roof, the water rose to her waist and, once again, a boat approached offering her rescue and safety and again she refused, steadfast in her faith that God would to come to her assistance.

Finally, the water rose so high that the woman was torn from her roof and she drowned. Upon her death, she found herself facing God for judgment and, with great indignation, confronted Him by saying "LORD, *I have been a good and faithful servant. I trusted in you and you failed to save me. You never responded to my pleas for help. Why, LORD, why?*" And God looked at the woman and said quietly, "*My dear one, I sent you three boats. What more did you need?*"

God always responds to our prayers. He never ignores our pleas. It is we who look for answers in the wrong places. We close our hearts and minds, waiting for God to respond directly and unequivocally to our desires. God seldom responds that way for He knows what is best for us, and therefore gives us what we need the most rather than what we most desire.

We really must look 'outside the box' if we wish to hear God's voice. God responds in echoes, reflections of sights and sounds, often obliquely and "*indistinctly, as in a mirror.*"[68] Wait for a voice coming from a cloud[69] and you will assuredly come face-to-face with God just as the woman did who passed on certain rescue three times.

---

[68] 1 Cor 13:12
[69] Mt 17:5

# It is a simple thing

There is an old proverb first attributed to John Heywood in 1562 which states, *"Out of sight, out of mind."*[70] It is a simple thing to ignore God. He created us, gave us free will, and then stepped aside so that He might enjoy the show. God showed us all that He had created and gave us dominion over it. God is not and never has been a nag or a scold. He has, for the most part, left us to our own devices. He placed us in charge of His creation, told us to take care of it, manage it, and to be good stewards of His bounty. But I'm sure that there have been moments when He has wondered whether He has perhaps made a serious mistake.

We lead busy lives and often we become so enamored with living that we forget to even acknowledge God's presence. We forget to speak or listen to Him; we simply ignore Him. But God is never too busy. God never ignores us nor does He forget us. But every now and then, He gets tired of being ignored and forgotten, and it is then that He steps into our lives in ways that are both unexpected and direct.

A number of years ago, I had the opportunity to spend a few hours with a family friend, someone whom I had not seen in nearly forty years. I had last seen Father John when I was twelve years old. At that time, he was a young Korean priest

---

[70] John Heywood, This proverb was first attributed to him around 1562 but it has been used by many others since that time. Its exact origin is unknown.

who was a gifted pianist with a marvelous voice. A few years later, Father John became a quadriplegic as a result of a diving accident. When I found that he had returned to my home town, I felt compelled to see him whenever the first opportunity presented itself.

For much of the intervening years, I had ignored God for far more important matters had demanded my attention. But God had grown tired of my recalcitrance. He took control, and I had no choice but to meet Him head-on.

As you might well imagine, forty years will change the physical appearance of a small boy. Not only was I taller and heavier, but I sported a beard and long hair and age had added more than a few lines and wrinkles to my face. Yet the moment I entered Father John's room, he greeted me with a smile and called me by name. It was instant recognition. He knew me. He knew before I ever uttered a single word all of who I had been and had become. And I knew that I was in the presence of more than a simple priest living in a broken body.

We never spoke of my lost faith; we only spoke of pleasant memories. As I prepared to leave, he gave me a book that he thought might *"help me on my journey."* And so it did. But what I found within its pages failed to compare with the eyes that burned into my soul, and the voice that spoke of forgiveness and love. I can offer no proof or submit any validation, but I know that God was there before me. I may have ignored Him for years, but He was there within my sight and will be forever in my mind. I was both humbled and ashamed, but all I felt in return was forgiveness and love.

# Look into the eyes of a stranger

You have undoubtedly been told or heard it said that you should look for the face of Jesus in everyone you meet. So how is that working out for you? I suspect that most of us would have some difficulty in recognizing him, even if he stood directly in front of us wearing a name tag, holding a placard, and displaying his signature stigmata. We believe. We really do. But …

The problem is that we hold an idealized image of Jesus and no one can measure up. We also decidedly miss the point. Jesus told us, *"behold, I am with you always, until the end of the age."*[71]

So if Jesus is with me always, he must be with you always. And if he is with you always, he must be with your neighbor, and his neighbor, and her neighbor, and so on.

My visit with Father John, a long-time family friend, convinced me beyond any doubt that I had been in the presence of Jesus. I had not one shred of doubt that I had looked into God's eyes and heard His voice. When I touched and hugged my friend, I knew that I had physically held Him in my arms.

---

[71] Mt 28:20

To say it was a sanctifying and humbling moment would be more than an understatement.

But Father John didn't look at all like the mental image I had of Jesus. And no, Father John isn't Jesus. For one thing, he is Korean not Jewish. Is he a holy man? Without any doubt. Is he a saint? Most certainly, at least within my own mind he is. But in truth, he is a normal human being, flesh and blood, and definitely not God. But at that moment when I really needed God, when I needed His presence so desperately, He filled my friend with Himself while opening my heart and my mind and I saw God. I saw Jesus looking back at me from the broken body of a friend.

I would like to say that my life changed completely that day, but that would be untrue. Oh, it changed for sure, just not as suddenly or as fully as one might expect. It is amazing how resistant we can become to change even when we know it is for the better. I fought God for a long time, stubbornly refusing to listen to His voice.

It was several years before I found myself no longer able to resist. I remember that day as if it were today. I was alone when I happened upon a poem that I had read years before but had long since forgotten.

As I read, it brought new meaning to me. While a lengthy poem, it was the first few lines that jarred my senses and gave me the nudge I needed.

It began:

*I fled Him, down the nights and down the days;*
  *I fled Him, down the arches of the years;*
*I fled Him, down the labyrinthine ways*
  *Of my own mind; and in the mist of tears*
*I hid from Him, and under running laughter.*
  *Up vistaed hopes I sped; And shot, precipitated*
*Adown Titanic glooms of chasmed fears,*
  *From those strong feet that followed after, followed after.*
*But with unhurrying case, and unperturbed pace,*
  *Deliberate speed, majestic instancy,*
*They beat — and a Voice beat more instant than the feet —*
  *"All things betray thee, who betrayest Me."*

That poem, THE HOUND OF HEAVEN by Francis Thompson,[72] spoke volumes to me. God spoke and I finally listened.

It is true. Look into the eyes of a stranger and you will see, listen to the voice of a friend and you will hear, touch the face of someone you love and you will find … God.

# When I heard His voice

I cannot recall the first time I heard God's voice just as no one ever remembers the moment of their birth. At birth, the cognitive abilities that will increase as we age are primitive and sufficient only to support life. Yet within moments, we are capable of reacting to external stimuli. We recognize a loving embrace. We hear a soothing voice and we smile. Instinctively,

---

[72] Francis Thompson, The Hound of Heaven, 1859-1907.

we know love even though we have no true understanding of its meaning. Comprehension and understanding are beyond the newness of our minds and quite simply beyond our capacity to know. It is a mystery and a truth so big, it cannot be exhausted in the knowing.

Unlike God, we are temporal creatures limited by space and time with human weaknesses and limitations. Our eyes are limited to seeing only visible light, a small portion of the electromagnetic spectrum; for there is far more that we cannot see than what we have the ability to see. Our ears are capable of hearing sound between 20-20,000 Hertz, although generally we hear a much smaller range (1000-5000 Hertz). Sounds beyond 20,000 Hertz exist, but we cannot hear them.

What all this means is that if we are to hear God's voice, we must overcome or set aside our innate human limitations and tune ourselves to His frequency and His light. When we were born, we felt loved without understanding. We did not try to analyze or intellectualize what we felt because we had no means to do so, just as we had neither the desire nor compulsion to go beyond the sense of well-being and nurturing love that surrounded us. We just felt loved and it was a good feeling.

So it is with God. In our humanity, our physical bodies, we cannot hear or see God, but through our spirituality, our souls, we can reach out and hear His voice.

71

While I cannot recall when God first began to speak to me, nor the second, third, or nth occasion, I can remember when I first became receptive to listening to what He had to say. And in retrospect, I have firm memories of moments when I chose to follow a certain path simply because I *heard* His voice whispering within my soul.

Not too long ago, I was asked to develop a timeline of my life. Wide latitude was given to its form. It could be a simple line marked with tics or dots to denote important events or it could be a meandering line full of curves and course corrections. What came to mind for me was a room filled with an endless number of colored balls each touching a myriad of other balls.

I saw my life as a journey through that room, neither straight nor level, coming in contact with so many. Every touch influenced my choices, and each had an impact on the path I would ultimately follow. At times, the going was easy, such as when I saw myself swimming above the sea of balls. When I sank below the surface, the way was slow and difficult.

God speaks to us in those moments when we need a gentle nudge, a soft caress, a tender touch. He speaks in our imagination, through circumstances, by others, and sometimes He speaks within our soul. When He does, it is usually best simply to shut up and listen.

# A driving force

I distinctly remember the day and the hour, the place and the circumstances when God made it known to me in a very emphatic way that He had had enough of my stubborn recalcitrance. It was an unusually pleasant Saturday in early January nearing noon. In the process of moving and starting a new business, I was temporarily on my own. My wife had yet to make the move, choosing to remain in our previous home until it had sold.

Shortly before noon that day, I left my apartment with the intention of doing some necessary shopping. As I neared the exit to the store, I found myself unable to make the turn. It was as if a force far stronger than I was in control. Invisible hands were at the wheel and I could do nothing but surrender to it. I vividly recall experiencing a tremendous pain at the back of my head as if it had been hammered by a baseball bat and I heard a voice – I am absolutely convinced it was Jesus – telling me *"Go to church, you fool!"*

Somehow I found myself in the parking lot of a nearby church. It was midday Saturday and the parking lot was completely empty, so I had every intention of simply driving through. But God had other ideas. After parking outside the parish office, I approached the entrance fully expecting to find a locked door. Instead, to my complete surprise, I found the door wide-open, and as I entered, I was met by an elderly, white-haired, portly gentleman wearing what appeared to be rather worn work clothes. I assumed that he was either the maintenance man or the janitor.

He asked if he could assist me, and I responded that I wasn't quite sure why I was there, that as ridiculous as it might sound, "*God made me do it!*" God had compelled me to come and had driven me to this spot.

We sat and talked for quite some time, several hours as it turned out to be. I told him of my distant and strained relationship with God, of my disillusionment with His church, of the feeling of emptiness in my life that I had been experiencing, and of a growing compulsion to rekindle my relationship with God. And while I spoke, he listened. Occasionally he would offer a few words of quiet encouragement and acceptance.

As the afternoon wore on, he suddenly glanced at the clock on the wall and hurriedly excused himself stating that he was late for an appointment. I left with him, and as I drove away, I recalled that he had told me that confessions were scheduled for three o'clock with Mass at four.

Incredible as it might sound, I once again found God forcefully driving me toward the confessional, and I found myself entering a church for the first time in many years. When it was my turn, I entered the confessional, and as I knelt, I realized that the man behind the curtain was the same person with whom I had spent the past few hours in conversation. He was neither the maintenance man nor the janitor but rather, as it turned out, a priest and the pastor no less.

Afterwards, as I knelt before the tabernacle offering penance to God, I experienced an overwhelming feeling of joy and relief. Just before leaving the confessional, the priest had asked, "*It feels pretty good, doesn't it?*"[73] And it did. It felt as if an enormous weight had been lifted away, so much so, that if I did not hold onto something solid, I would simply float away.

The joy I felt was greater than one experiences when reunited with a loved one after a long absence, greater than seeing a loved one whom you thought you would never see again. I felt His loving embrace surrounding me, holding me, gently wiping away my tears. I heard Him say, "*All is forgiven*" and "*I have always loved you and will love you always.*" As sinful as I had been, and though a sinner I would continue to be, I knew I had been unconditionally and with great love welcomed home.

I remained there for a long time and attended the Mass that followed, during which I experienced an almost overwhelming sensation of God's love and forgiveness throughout the liturgy. The Eucharistic celebration – the Mass – was exhilarating and so unlike what I remembered from my youth. Every word, every song, every action only served to increase my deepest sorrow for the years of loss, and yet I felt

---

[73] After nearly a dozen years, I can still hear Father Simpson's words as if it were yesterday.

renewed, filled with so much of God's love and His divine mercy.

As the priest held the host above the chalice and invited us to express our unworthiness and ask for His forgiveness with the words, *"LORD I am not worthy to receive you but only say the word and my soul shall be healed,"*[74] my body shook with a terrible emotion. With full awareness and absolute clarity, I was overcome with *agapé*, the unconditional love that God has for each of us, and all I could do was tremble at the thought that my soul would be healed if only I should ask. That sensation remains with me to this very day.

# Responding to God's call

Most of us have received at least one formal invitation in our lives; most likely to some significant event such as a wedding, ordination, banquet, or graduation. Generally these invitations have four letters printed on them — RSVP — which is the abbreviation for the French phrase *"répondez s'il vous plaît"* or *"please respond."* Common courtesy dictates that, when we receive such an invitation, we should respond as soon as

---

[74] This was the people's response at the elevation of the Eucharist during Mass. The third edition of the Roman Missal, English Edition, which was instituted at the beginning of Advent, 2010, modified this to be *"Lord, I am not worthy that you should enter under my roof, but only say the word and my soul shall be healed."* The older version was the one currently in use on the occasion of my return to the faith.

possible indicating our acceptance or refusal so that the host can ascertain how many will be attending.

God calls each of us by name and invites us to do His will, but I often wonder just how many of us ever bother to respond to His invitation.

Many of us never hear His call because we surround ourselves with too much noise; too many voices — including our own — drowning out any chance that we might have to hear God's voice. And, like Elijah, we all too often expect God to call us in a loud voice like a strong and heavy wind or an earthquake or fire. But, as you may recall, God's voice was in a tiny whispering sound[75] and that requires us to open our hearts and minds, to turn up our spiritual hearing aids, and to put ourselves in a place where we can hear His voice. But above all else, we must listen because when we listen, we will hear His voice calling us to follow Him.

Sometimes we hear His call but feel unworthy or not up to the task that He is asking us to do. But — and this is terribly important and essential to understand — when God calls, you should always respond. You may recall that when Jonah refused God's call the first time,[76] he ended up tossed overboard and into the belly of a whale. When God called him a second time, he never hesitated but answered the call immediately and

---

[75] 1 Kgs 19:11-12.
[76] Jon 1:1-15.

both his life and those of Nineveh were transformed, changed forever.

Jesus called his apostles when he said, *"Come after me, and I will make you fishers of men."*[77] Who were those who he called? Were they the pillars of the community, the wealthy or the powerful? No. They were ordinary people without wealth or position, with no special education, no social or political standing. They were ordinary people. Most were fishermen and one was even a tax collector. All were sinners who immediately accepted His call. They simply dropped everything and followed him.

When we are called by God to serve, we need to understand that He will never ask us to do more than what we are capable of doing. Neither should we believe that we have nothing to offer. If we place our trust in God, He will guide us through the darkest times and show us the way with His light.

When God calls it can be traumatic; it almost certainly will be life-changing. Often you may not be prepared or you may be reluctant to respond. You always have a choice: you may either ignore His call or open yourself to His will. The difficulty lies in realizing that if you do say "yes", your life will be changed forever. You will be a new person and the future will always remain unknown.

---

[77] Mk 1:17.

As for myself, I heard that tiny whispering sound for over thirty years, but stubbornly refused to listen. It was always there but I was too busy with life to acknowledge God's call. What I did not realize until much later was that, like Jonah, I had been tossed overboard into the belly of the beast. But, unlike Jonah, rather than three days, it took thirty years before I was spewed from the belly of the beast and knew God's mercy. When God called a second time, it was as if He took a baseball bat to the back of my head and — like Jonah — I did not refuse to hear His call the second time.

We must understand that God is outside of time or, as Saint Peter wrote, *"With the LORD a day is like a thousand years, and a thousand years are like a day."*[78] What to us is a very long time is quite literally no time at all to God. He is infinitely patient and willing to give us all the time in the world to respond to Him. What we must do, all that we are required to do, is to place our trust in Him, know that He loves us, and that He will give us all the gifts and grace we need to do His will.

Accepting God's call is seldom easy. There will always be obstacles and difficulties placed before us. But as long as we place ourselves in His hands, we can be assured that He will be there to see us through the rough spots.

At my ordination to the Permanent Diaconate, I became a new person. I truly do not recognize who I was before. I can neither rationally nor adequately explain it, except to say that I

---

[78] 2 Pt 3:8.

was transformed by the Holy Spirit into this new me. I often feel guilty for all the joy I receive in serving Him in such a poor way. I only regret that I did not listen when He first called out to me so long ago. All the joy and blessings that I have missed simply because I refused to listen; I failed to place my trust in Him, believing that I was in control and that I was the master of my own destiny.

We have this natural inclination to believe that when things are going well it is of our own choosing, but when difficult times arise we look to God and ask *"Why?"* We are quick to believe that God has deliberately and intentionally placed obstacles in our path, and we want Him to remove them so that we can continue blissfully on our way. What we fail to understand is that God's path is the easy one and that it is we who create the difficulties along the journey by not putting our faith in God and giving control of our lives over to Him.

A few years ago, I was diagnosed with a serious health issue that called for major surgery. While I was told that I had a good heart, some of my plumbing urgently needed major repair. This would require splitting me open, stopping my heart, replacing a portion of my aorta with a piece of garden hose, and then attempting to restart my engine with an ignition system that had only been used once more than sixty-five years before.

To say that I was a wee bit nervous would be an understatement. A few weeks before my scheduled surgery, after a restless and sleepless night filled with cold sweats and panic attacks, I presided at an early morning Communion Service. It was difficult for me to focus on the service until at the Responsorial Psalm, we responded *"In God I trust..."*[79] Upon hearing and saying those words, all my anxiety and fears immediately and completely left me. I realized at that moment that God had a plan for me and that I was not in control. He was and He is.

I was in that instant and continue to remain at peace knowing that He has been and always will be with me, beside me, around me, and within me. I realized that He had waited patiently for me to listen to His call and to *"répondez s'il vous plait,"* and that He had much more in store for me to do. I felt so very blessed by His love and the love of those around me, and I discovered, perhaps later than most, that that is more than enough.

---

[79] Ps 56:11.

# Part II

Seek and you will find

# You

O LORD, God and Master of all creation,
     all glory and honor is yours.
You have given us the grace of life,
     and the gifts to hear your voice.
You have made us in your image and
     placed within us an eternal sanctuary
     where only two can dwell.
We listen for your Word, your Voice;
     open our hearts, our minds to you.
Open our eyes and ears to hear your voice,
     so that we may follow faithfully
and live lives of grace and saintliness.

# Chapter Five

## In the beginning

*In the beginning, when God created*
*the heavens and the earth ...*

*God said:*
*"Let us make man in our image,*
*after our likeness.*
*Let them have dominion over*
*the fish of the sea, the birds of the air,*
*and the cattle, and over all the wild animals and*
*all the creatures that crawl on the ground.*

*God created man in his image,*
*in the divine image He created him;*
*male and female He created them.*

Gen 1:1, 26-27

# The Word of God

The English word *Bible* comes from the Greek *ta biblia* which means "The Books," a name well-chosen, since the Bible is a collection of many individual works and not the product of a single writer. Year after year, the Bible remains the world's largest selling book, averaging thirty million copies a year—perhaps one hundred and fifty billion in all since Gutenberg invented the printing press in 1453.[80]

The Bible, or Sacred Scripture as it is often called, is recognized by all Christians as the Word of God. Note the use of the singular "Word." It is never the "Words of God." Saint Paul tells us that, through all the written words contained within Sacred Scripture, God speaks only one single Word, His one Utterance in whom He expresses Himself completely.[81] And Saint Augustine wrote, *"You recall that one and the same Word of God extends throughout Scripture, that it is one and the same Utterance that resounds in the mouths of all the sacred writers, since He who was in the beginning God with God has no need of separate syllables; for He is not subject to time."*[82]

God has spoken to mankind from the very beginning and continues to speak to us through His Word. While the Bible in all its forms and versions has had more copies published than

---

[80] Lawrence Boadt, CSP, *Reading the Old Testament: An Introduction; Second Edition*, 2012, Paulist Press.
[81] CCC 102, Cf. Heb 1:1-3.
[82] CCC 102, Saint Augustine, *Enarrationes in Psalmos*.

any other book, exactly how many of those copies have been actually read and studied is altogether a separate issue. All too often, the Bible finds a home on a bookshelf or table where it gathers dust and remains forever unopened and unread.

Our inability to hear God's voice is not only a mere reluctance to listen with our ears; it is compounded by our refusal to listen with all our senses. We see with blinders only what we wish to see, filtering out all that we do not.

It makes no sense to admire a sunset in the dark of night; no one lights a lamp and then covers it with a bushel basket;[83] neither can we absorb or hear the Word of God by studying the cover of Sacred Scripture. The fullness of the Word of God cannot be expressed in a tweet, nor can it be condensed or abbreviated. It is, in its completeness, God's message to His creation, and there can be no abridged edition that contains His Word.

From the beginning of time until the birth of Jesus, Sacred Scripture outlined human history and described the relationship between man and God, and specifically between the people of Israel and Yahweh/God.

It is the narrative of God, always faithful, and His relationship with man, much less so. It is an anthology of myth, history, prose, poetry, and song that spans more than six billion

---

[83] Mt 5:15.

years of God's unwavering love for his creation and humanity's almost constant vacillation in their devotion to their creator.

Biblical scholars believe that the books of the Old Testament are an amalgamation of ancient texts and traditions taken from at least four sources, each with their own perspectives, understandings, biases, and agenda. Six billion years is a long time, especially when we consider that the earliest evidence of a true written language is a mere five thousand years into our past. Most of the history of man is therefore lost and unrecoverable, at least to the degree of certainty that modern historians and scholars believe to be necessary. To accept and believe in the Word of God, therefore, requires a rational mind, fervent devotion, and faith in God.

From the beginning, God has communicated with all His creation through many different voices. Different voices were the most appropriate for reaching stubborn, recalcitrant creatures, creatures who often have considered themselves quite capable of existence without God.

Although God is unknowable to our temporal minds, it is impossible to calculate all the ways that He has chosen to express His desires for every human heart. It is for us to be open to receive His Word in whatever form or manner, and for us to be receptive to His message.

If we are to understand God's Word as inscribed by men upon the pages of Sacred Scripture, we must do so with more than a casual eye. Anyone who wishes to hear God's Word must address the singularity of that single Utterance rather than selectively parsing the written words transcribed by man. We must, of human necessity, listen and absorb His Word in manageable portions, and that presents challenges to our ability to fully hear and completely comprehend His Word. But so long as we strive to absorb all that God desires, we will receive all that He intends.

Written upon the pages of the books of the Old Testament, we hear God speak in many ways to many people. In the beginning, God speaks to the void as described in the first chapter of Genesis when He created the heavens and the earth and saw the earth filled with everything that was good. Then *"God created man in his image, in the divine image He created him; male and female He created them."*[84] And He commanded man, *"You are free to eat from any of the trees of the garden except the tree of knowledge of good and bad. From that tree you shall not eat; the moment you eat from it you are surely doomed to die."*[85]

Even though man frequently failed to follow His command, God continued to communicate with his often wayward creation, at times directly, at other times through dreams and visions, often through angels, messengers, visitors, and prophets, and occasionally through visible signs and images.

---

[84] Gn 1:27.
[85] Gn 2:16-17.

We can find many instances of these voices within the pages of the Old Testament. God spoke directly with Noah, Abram, Isaac, and Jacob/Israel. He spoke to Abram as a vision and Abram, Isaac, Jacob/Israel within dreams. He sent angels, messengers, and visitors to Abram, Lot, and Jacob/Israel. He spoke through the prophets, prophets such as Elijah, Job, Johan, Hosea, and Isaiah. He used visible signs such as the parting of the Red Sea, the raining down bread from heaven, speaking from the dense cloud, and the burning bush.

But far more important than the methods through which God chose to speak to His creation was, and is, the message that He wishes to convey. And, for the most part, it is straightforward and easily understood. You will find His message in two books of the Torah[86]: Exodus[87] and Deuteronomy.[88] Jesus would subsequently confirm this when he said,

> *You shall love the LORD, your God, with all your heart,*
> *with all your soul, and with all your mind. This is the*
> *greatest and the first commandment. The second is like*
> *it: You shall love your neighbor as yourself. The whole*

---

[86] The Torah (Hebrew: תּוֹרָה, "Instruction", "Teaching"), or the Pentateuch is Judaism's most important text. It is composed of the Five Books of Moses (the first five books of the Bible) and also contains the 613 commandments (מִצְוֹת, mitzvot) and the Ten Commandments.
[87] Ex 20:1-17.
[88] Dt 5:6-21.

*law and the prophets depend on these two commandments.*[89]

# The Timelessness of God

*"Get behind me, Satan. You are thinking not as God does, but as human beings do."*[90] In his rebuke of Peter, Jesus was making the point that God is beyond our understanding, beyond our knowing. It is not for us to question God for we are His creatures, created in His image to love and to serve Him.

Our physical lives are measured by the passage of time, a steady beat, second by second, moment by moment, day by day, that begins at the moment of conception and continues only for as long as God has determined it should be. Each second of our life lasts exactly as long as the prior one, and one second two-thousand years ago lasted exactly the same as one second today.

We see time as a linear concept inexorably moving from one moment to the next, never slowing nor stopping, always moving forward, never back. We see the past as memories of what has been, the future as visions of what might become, but we live in the now.

The speed of light is 186,282 miles per second. In 1905, Albert Einstein introduced his Special Theory of Relativity which declared a law for all motion. Einstein posited that the

---

[89] Mt 22:37-39.
[90] Mk 8:33.

combined speed of any object's motion through space and its motion through time is always precisely equal to the speed of light. Since light waves use all of their motion to travel through space at light speed, they have absolutely no motion through time.

Thus every photon that has ever been produced exists in an ageless state. Or, more simply put, the universe ages but light does not. Scientists tell us that we can approach, but never travel as fast as or faster than, the speed of light. They have also proven that as a body approaches the speed of light time slows down inversely relative to the speed of travel.

Science has also proven the existence and nature of "black holes" which, rather than being empty space, consists of a great amount of matter packed into a very small area – imagine a star ten times more massive than the Sun squeezed into a sphere approximately the diameter of New York City – resulting in a gravitational field so strong that nothing, not even light, can escape and thus time within it stands still.

We are temporal creatures. We are conceived, born, live, and eventually die, ever at the steady beat of time. And it is precisely for that reason that we cannot understand or know God for He exists outside of time. We may glimpse the variability of time through greater understanding of the speed of light and black holes, but that tells us nothing of the timelessness or the nature of God.

To God, every time is now. There is no past, present, or future. There is only the eternal now. God told Moses " אֶהְיֶה אֲשֶׁר אֶהְיֶה, 'ehyeh 'ašer 'ehyeh, I AM WHO AM,"[91] a clear statement of His eternal nature, ever being, without beginning, without end. And it is His timeless nature that most prevents us from truly knowing God, for it defies all temporal and scientific understanding. We speak of eternity as a very long time, but the truth is: It is not time at all.

# To know God

Today, more so than at any time in the long history of man, there are those who have convinced themselves that God is knowable and that to understand the nature and composition of God, all one must do is delve deeper to fully comprehend truth in the absolute. Such arrogance and conceit in the minds of the created know few bounds. Surely God enjoys the encounter with such foolishness, recognizing the futility in such endeavors and the realization that the joke is completely lost on the unwise.

The difficulty in putting God in His place is, of course, that He is everywhere and nowhere, all-time and no-time. Saint Thomas Aquinas described God as the *"Source who has no Source,"*[92] meaning that God has no beginning and has no end. He has always existed. He has never been out of existence.

---

[91] Ex 3:14.
[92] Saint Thomas Aquinas, *Summa Theologiciae.*

Nothing caused God into being because nothing caused God to be.

Those who deny the existence of God often pose the question, *"If everything needs a cause, then what caused God?"* While current scientific evidence strongly suggests that, at some point in time, the universe began to exist, there is no corresponding moment when God began to exist because He is eternally timeless and not constrained by our limited notion of time. For, in truth, God created the universe and time itself.

An article written by Trent Horn provides an excellent overview of the evidence for the creation of the universe and God's relationship to its causation. Horn offers this insight in answer to the question, *"If the universe began to exist, what was God doing during the eternity before the world began?"*

> *Saint Augustine confronted this question in the fifth century. His joking response was that for all eternity God was making hell for people who ask questions like this (Confessions, 229). His more serious response was that prior to the creation of the world there was no time. It makes no sense to ask what God was doing prior to the creation of the world, because the creation of the world included the first moment in time.*[93]

---

[93] Trent Horn, *The Heavens Declare the Glory of God: How the universe provides evidence for the existence of God*, Catholic Answers Magazine, March/April 2014.

Those who admit the existence of God but believe He can be identified, quantified, measured, and defined – that is, placed into a well-confined box – are arguing from both sides of the same coin. They admit to God's existence while containing Him within circumscribed limits, thus reducing God to less than God, proffering the argument in support of a demigod who, like the rest of creation, is existential and thus relegated to time and space. Arguably, this god might indeed be knowable, but then this notion of god is not God.

I do not know God – but I know that God exists. How do I explain this knowing? Meister Eckhart said it well:

> *The whole Being of God is contained in God alone. The whole of humanity is not contained in one man, for one man is not all men. But in God the soul knows all humanity, and all things at their highest level of existence, since it knows them in their essence....Thus I am as sure, as I am of my own existence and God's that, if the soul is to know God, it must know Him outside of time and place.*[94]

The truth that we cannot know God does not negate His existence. God loves and that is enough.

---

[94] Justs Junkulis, *10 Jewels of Christian Mysticism: A Selection of Western Tradition Primary Texts*, "Meister Eckhart's Sermons" by Johannes Eckhart, Sermon II, The Nearness of the Kingdom, 2013.

# To love God is to know God

In describing how we can know how near we are to the Kingdom of God, Meister Eckhart tells us:

*If I were a king, and did not know it, I should not really be a king. But, if I were fully convinced that I was a king, and all of mankind coincided in my belief, and I knew that they shared my conviction, I should indeed be a king, and all the wealth of the king would be mine. But, if one of these three conditions were lacking, I should not really be a king.*[95]

In other words, if I know a thing to be true and you also know the truth of it, and I know that you know it to be true, then it must be true. But, conversely, if either I do not know a thing to be true or you do not know the truth of it, or I do not know that you know it to be true, then it must not be true.

While there is some obvious logic to this argument, it is not without its fault; for it presupposes that what we know and understand to be true is, in fact, the truth. If all know that a thing is true which is, in fact, false then my awareness of your knowledge of the truth can never transform the falsity of it into the truth.

All this is in continuation of what I previously declared by stating that *"I do not know God – but I know that God exists."* Or

---

[95] Ibid.

as the anonymous writer of the Cloud of Unknowing tells his pupil, *"God cannot be grasped with our minds, only by our love,"* and later writes, *"As long as I am a soul living in a mortal body, I will always see and feel this heavy cloud of unknowing between me and God."*[96]

There are many forms of knowing, many types of knowledge, and numerous definitions for the word. It is far too easy to miss the truth when your perception and acceptance of it comes from a different perspective or context.

One can say that *'to know'* means *'to perceive directly'* or to *'to have a practical understanding of, as through experience; be skilled in'* and, if that is your understanding of the term, then clearly since *"[n]o one has ever seen God,"*[97] no one can *'know'* God.

Another use of the word, although archaic, is *'to know someone in the conjugal sense'* and this most definitely does not apply to any knowledge of God.

No one truly *'knows'* another for no one can *'know'* what lies within the heart of another. This applies whether someone is a complete stranger or a beloved spouse with whom you have spent a life-time in *'knowing.'* If you are incapable of *'knowing'* another human being whom you love, how can you ever assume that you could *'know'* God? As you can never completely know your beloved, all the more so you can never know God.

---

[96] Carmen Acevedo Butcher, *The Cloud of Unknowing: A New Translation*, 2011.
[97] 1 Jn 4:12.

There is yet another meaning for 'knowing' that comes closer to what I meant, and is of far greater import and that is this: as created beings, we cannot formulate or calculate who or what God is. No one can describe God's appearance, nor can He be measured or quantified, for God cannot be contained and confined within any theology or etymology.

We can state, affirm, and prove that God does exist but God is beyond our understanding. *"God is great beyond our knowledge."*[98]

Again the anonymous master writes:

*Nothing can really be said about God. No single noun, verb, or any other part of speech can describe him. Why do we expect visible signs to be able to articulate the invisible nature of God?*[99]

Elsewhere he tells his pupil:

*I know you'll ask me 'How do I think on God as God, and who is God?' and I can only answer, 'I don't know'...That's why I'm willing to abandon everything I know, to love the one thing I cannot think. He can be loved, but not thought.*[100]

The truth is: to love God is to know God ... and that is all we need to know.

---

[98] Job 36:26.
[99] Carmen Acevedo Butcher, *The Cloud of Unknowing: A New Translation*, 2011.
[100] Ibid.

# In His image and likeness

In the beginning – before the beginning – God in His infinite and boundless perfection created angels, archetypes of the soul, immortal spirits *"stamped with the seal of perfection, of complete wisdom and perfect beauty."*[101] God, who is all good and beyond all perfection, brought them into existence and gave them gifts beyond imagining and placed them on His holy mountain, *"in Eden, the garden of God."*[102] And the first of these was Lucifer, who was known as the morning star and the son of the dawn.

Yet for all his power and favor with God, Lucifer was dissatisfied and he said, *"I will scale the heavens; above the stars of God I will set up my throne; I will take my seat on the Mount of Assembly, in the recesses of the North. I will ascend above the tops of the clouds; I will be like the Most High!"*[103] Thus God's magnificent creation fell to the temptation of desiring more, of desiring to be more than he was, and so God reduced Lucifer and his followers to dust on the earth, and transformed them into ghastly horrors eternally devoured by fire.[104]

Then God in His omnipotence and wisdom desired into being a new and temporal universe, and filled it with natural beauty and wondrous creatures. And then God created man –

---

[101] Ez 28:12.
[102] Ez 28:13
[103] Is 14:13-14.
[104] Ez 28:18-19.

like angels, only more – for God said, *"Let us make man in our image, after our likeness,"*[105] and so God *"formed man out of the clay of the ground and blew into his nostrils the breath of life, and so man became a living being."*[106] But God's new creation was more than living clay, for God breathed into man a soul, an immortal spirit as are angels. And God *"planted a garden in Eden, in the east, and He placed there the man whom He had formed"*[107] and the man was called *Adam* which in ancient Hebrew means *'man.'*

God created a kindred soul called woman for Adam and gave them dominion over all living things and gave them this command: *"You are free to eat from any of the trees of the garden except the tree of knowledge of good and bad."*[108] And yet despite God's unbounded largesse, man was dissatisfied and easily tempted by the serpent who said, *"You certainly will not die! No, God knows well that the moment you eat of it your eyes will be opened and you will be like gods who know what is good and what is bad."*[109] And so, filled with the desire for more, of being more than they were, man and woman ate it and *"the eyes of both of them were opened, and they realized that they were naked"*[110]

As Thomas Merton once noted, *"There is no evil in anything created by God, nor can anything of His become an obstacle*

---

[105] Gn 1:26.
[106] Gn 2:7.
[107] Gn 2:8.
[108] Gn 2:16-17.
[109] Gn 3:4-5.
[110] Gn 3:7.

*to our union with Him.*"[111] God created both angels and men out of His inestimable and unquenchable love and, because of His love, He endowed them with free will, the ability to make their own decisions, knowing fully that some would choose unwisely and even wrongly. Yet God could do no less, for He desired only love in return and knew that forced love was no love at all.

## The unthinkable separation from God

After man and woman ate of the forbidden fruit, "*the eyes of both of them were opened, and they realized that they were naked; so they sewed fig leaves together and made loincloths for themselves.*"[112]

There can be little doubt that neither man nor woman understood the serious and long-lasting ramifications of their simple act of defiance nor disobedience to God's will. After God created woman, we read "*The man and his wife were both naked, yet they felt no shame,*"[113] but when our first parents acted against the direct command of God and ate the fruit from the tree of knowledge of good and bad, their eyes were opened and they felt shame.

And it is by their new sight that we have been tormented since the beginning, for God never meant for man to know evil; rather He made man out of His inestimable love desiring only man's love in return.

---

[111] Thomas Merton, New Seeds of Contemplation, 1961.
[112] Gn 3:7.
[113] Gn 2:25.

One way to better understand this is to look at the very young. They harbor no inhibitions. They neither understand the concept of nakedness nor do they have a conscious knowledge of good or bad. Everything is new, waiting to be explored and experienced.

There is no right or wrong, good or bad, joy or sorrow. There is only the undiscovered and the yet to be experienced "new". That is until someone reaches out and tells them, "*no, that is forbidden.*" And when they disregard that taboo — and at some point they always do — and suffer for their disobedience, their eyes are opened and they understand. If only they had listened and obeyed.

It is somewhat of a paradox and certainly ironic that, when man's eyes were opened, he lost the ability to see clearly, to distinguish between the good and the bad. God had given him dominion over all that was good and had forbidden only that which was not. Yet man coveted that of which he had neither knowledge nor understanding, and ate it based upon the meretricious guile of the serpent, the master of lies and deceit. If only man had listened and obeyed God.

Because of man's disobedience God said, "*See! The man has become like one of us, knowing what is good and what is bad! Therefore, he must not be allowed to put out his hand to take fruit from the tree of life also, and thus eat of it and live forever.*"[114] And so God expelled man from the garden and away from the tree of life.

---

[114] Gn 3:22.

The price that man paid for his disobedience and his sin was death and separation from God for no longer could man see or hear God as before.

What was lost was far greater than just life in the Garden of Eden, although that was indeed a considerable loss, but the greatest loss was the unthinkable separation from God's presence and voice. When man's eyes were opened, God distanced Himself from man, removing Himself from man's direct sight and hearing. It was as if God had placed Himself behind a one-way mirror. God loved his creation and, therefore, remained ever watchful but man, for the first time, experienced a deep sense of loss and abandonment. For the first time, he now realized that he was truly alone. He had been left to fend for himself and to choose what was right and what was not. Man had been weaned abruptly from the succor of God's presence and was now on his own.

Man now saw both the good and the bad. But as we are witnesses, man has often had great difficulty in discerning the difference. God knew that from before the beginning. Man did not. And the rest is history.

# Chapter Six

## In the beginning was the Word

*In the beginning was the Word,*
*and the Word was with God,*
*and the Word was God.*
*He was in the beginning with God.*
*All things came to be through him,*
*and without him nothing came to be.*
*What came to be through him was life,*
*and this life was the light of the human race;*
*the light shines in the darkness,*
*and the darkness has not overcome it.*

John 1:1-5

# I believe, help my unbelief

Do you believe in Jesus Christ? If so – and I sincerely trust that you do – what is it that you believe? These are not mere rhetorical inquiries nor are they intended to disparage or dismiss; rather they are posed to provoke and to call forth serious consideration of exactly who Jesus is and what he calls us to believe. Simple acceptance is insufficient, for Jesus demands that we not only believe in him but that we live in him, and that through our living, we bring testimony and glory to God the Father, Son, and Holy Spirit.

It is how we live our lives that give the truest reflection to how we might respond to the first question. Anyone can say, *"Yes, I believe in Jesus Christ,"* even while living a sinful life. Anyone can profess to be a Christian while ignoring all that is demanded of a true and faithful follower of our LORD and Savior. Anyone can live in and of the world while loudly and publicly proclaiming the Good News of Jesus Christ. Anyone can ... but then anyone can be *"a resounding gong or a clashing cymbal."*[115]

Jesus calls us to believe in him, to have faith in him just as we believe and have faith in God the Father. Throughout his public ministry, Jesus continually told his disciples – and therefore each of us – that everything he said and did came from the Father, and yet no matter how many times he

---

[115] 1 Cor 13:1.

professed his complete and total unity with God the Father, his disciples – both then and now – have shown great reluctance in understanding and believing the truth of it.

We see the man and hear his voice, but fail to connect the dots and to wed the human with the divine. Jesus said, "*The Father and I are one,*" and the Jews tried to stone him for they saw only a man proclaiming to be God rather than truly God in human form.[116]

We believe, yet we do not believe just as much as the father of the boy possessed by a demon cried out, "*I do believe, help my unbelief!*"[117] All too often it is our unbelief that overwhelms our belief, our head rebelling against our heart, the visible denying the invisible.

Jesus tells us that "*No one comes to the Father except through me. If you know me, then you will also know my Father*"[118] and, again, we fail to hear the Voice of God. We refuse to accept that it is God speaking and that the Father, Son, and Holy Spirit are indivisibly united in their Oneness. We still ask as Philip did, "*Master, show us the Father, and that will be enough for us,*"[119] and refuse to hear Jesus clearly and unequivocally reply, "*Whoever has seen me has seen the Father. How can you say 'Show us the*

---

[116] Jn 10:30-33.
[117] Mk 9:24.
[118] Jn 14:7.
[119] Jn 14:8.

*Father'? Do you not believe that I am in the Father and the Father is in me?"*[120]

It is only within your heart that you may know and respond to the question as to what you believe. Only you and God know what you do and do not believe, and that means you and God the Father, Son, and Holy Spirit.

# The Word became flesh

It has been suggested that the prologue to the Gospel of John[121] may have originated from an early Christian hymn. Regardless of its origin, the lyrical quality of its words captures the eternal preexistent essence and relationship of the incarnate *Logos* to God with near perfection. It is a beautiful psalm of praise to the Word become flesh, the incarnation of the unlimited Divine into the limited world of man.

What is lacking in this ode to the incarnate Word is the degree to which Jesus was both radical and transformative. Through his death and resurrection, he gave us a new covenant in his blood and brought salvation to us all. Through his life and public ministry he radically transformed man's relationship with God.

What has largely been ignored is just how radical was the historical Jesus, for he quite literally and inalterably changed the

---

[120] Jn 14:9-10.
[121] Jn 1:1-5, 10-11, 14.

108

human paradigm that had existed and had been developing over the broad span of man's existence. What is especially important to understand, indeed it is absolutely imperative that we do so, is that Jesus was and is truly the Voice of God. Every word, every interaction, every act of his was God in the divine person of the Son communicating directly with His creation.

When we read the Bible, both the old and the new, we discover all of the marvelous and mundane ways that God has communicated with those whom He created. But nowhere does God speak directly to the whole of creation except through the incarnated presence of His Son, Jesus Christ. John tells us, "*He was in the world, and the world came to be through him, but the world did not know him. He came to what was his own, but his own people did not accept him.*"[122] And the questions remain: do we still not know him and will we ever accept him?

We call ourselves Christians and followers of Jesus Christ, but what do we believe of him? There have been those who throughout history have claimed to be of divine origin and therefore divine – emperors, kings, pharaohs, and others – but all have been proven to be mere poseurs, actors upon the stage of life who have for the most part been quickly forgotten. Many religions follow great and revered men – Buddhists follow Buddha, Muslims follow Mohammed – but none have ever been considered to be God. Muslims and Jews consider Jesus to be a great prophet and a holy man, but do not accept or believe that

---

[122] Jn 1:10-11.

he was or is divine. As Christians, we are called to believe that Jesus was more than just a man, a holy man, or a prophet. We are called to believe that he was both fully human and fully divine and that he was the Son of God.

The First Council of Nicaea was convened in 325 A.D. by the Roman Emperor Constantine I in an effort to settle the Christological argument concerning the exact nature of Jesus, an argument that had been raging since the earliest days of the Church.

One position, supported by Saints Alexander of Alexandria and Athanasius, held that Jesus was the only begotten Son of the Father consubstantial with the Father. Another position, supported by the bishop Arius, promoted the idea that Jesus was created by God, a super creation above all other creatures, angels and man inclusive.

The Council, in a nearly unanimous decision (Arius and two others dissented and were subsequently anathematized, that is, excommunicated,) agreed with the first position and signed the document which we now know as the Nicene Creed. And it is from this document that we profess and believe that Jesus is one in being with the Father and the Holy Spirit. We acknowledge and affirm that Jesus Christ is God from God, Light from Light, and not a creation but the Creator of all things.

It is from the early church councils and the church fathers that we have come to believe and to understand what is written,

*"And the Word became flesh and made his dwelling among us, and we saw his glory, the glory as of the Father's only Son, full of grace and truth."*[123]

# Behold the man

"Ecce homo!" "Behold the man!"[124]

It is with these words that Pilate presented Jesus of Nazareth bound and crowned with thorns to the Jewish crowd just before he sent him away to be crucified.

Saint John tells us that *"No one has ever seen God"*[125] and yet our Christian faith calls this very statement into question. Although the New Testament contains numerous instances that illustrate the divinity of Christ, the issue was far from settled for many centuries after his death and resurrection.

The First Council of Nicaea defined and declared the divinity of Jesus Christ in direct response to the Arian heresy, which had taught that Christ was not divine but was rather a superhuman creature made by God.

The Ecumenical Councils of Nicaea in 325 A.D. and Constantinople in 381 A.D subsequently produced the Nicene Creed, the profession of faith through which we confirm our belief in *"Jesus Christ, the only begotten Son of God, born of the*

---

[123] Jn 1:14.
[124] Jn 19:5.
[125] 1 Jn 4:12.

111

*Father before all ages, God from God, Light from Light, true God from true God, begotten, not made, consubstantial with the Father."*[126]

At the Last Supper, Jesus told his disciples, *"I am the way and the truth and the life. No one comes to the Father except through me. If you know me, then you will also know my Father. From now on you do know him and have seen him."*[127] If what we profess as truth is indeed the truth and we firmly believe in our Lord Jesus Christ, then we must hold fast to the belief that Jesus is truly God. And from this we must profess that anyone who ever saw Jesus in the flesh did indeed see God, at least as manifested by the incarnation of His only Son.

So the question that remains for us to answer is how do you see Jesus? Do you see the man or do you see God? Our faith calls for us to see Jesus as both fully human and fully divine, having two natures, united with God in personhood with the Father and the Holy Spirit. It is a mystery beyond the capacity of man to comprehend or decipher and a mystery as confounding and unknowable as God Himself.

Thomas Merton once wrote, *"There is 'no such thing' as God because God is neither a 'what' nor a 'thing' but a pure 'who.'"*[128] Much the same can and should be said of Jesus Christ, for he is not a creature made by God but is God personified. He is the Word of God and *"In the beginning was the Word, and the Word*

---

[126] CCC 195.

[127] Jn 14:6-7.

[128] Thomas Merton, New Seeds of Contemplation, 1961.

*was with God, and the Word was God. He was in the beginning with God. All things came to be through him, and without him nothing came to be.*"[129]

Matthew tells us that "*Jesus went around to all the towns and villages, teaching in their synagogues, proclaiming the gospel of the kingdom, and curing every disease and illness.*"[130] Yet no miracle proved to be a greater sign of his divinity and divine power than his raising of Lazarus from the dead.

It is within the context of his divinity that we may come to better understand his apparent nonchalance when he received word from his friends Mary and Martha that their brother Lazarus was ill, for we read that "*he remained for two days where he was.*"[131]

Why did he delay? That is certainly the question that perplexed Mary and Martha when he finally arrived four days after Lazarus had died and had been buried.

While those who knew Jesus had come to believe that he was the Messiah, the Christ, the Son of God, no one, not even his closest friends, believed him to be divine. No one understood what he was saying when he told them, "*The Father and I are one.*"[132]

---

129 Jn 1:1-3.
130 Mt 9:35.
131 Jn 11:6.
132 John 10:30.

To fully comprehend how the disciples saw Jesus, we must first attempt to understand their beliefs in the context of their time and place.

Those who followed Jesus held widely different views of the terms *Messiah* and *Christ*. Christ or *Christós*, Χριστός is the ancient Greek word for the Hebrew מָשִׁיחַ (Māšîaḥ) and the Syriac ܡܫܝܚܐ (M'shiha). The word *messiah* simply means *anointed*, and those who were anointed were typically those kings and priests ordained by God to lead the nation of Israel.

Pheme Perkins, theology professor at Boston College and author of Reading the New Testament, points out that at the time when Jesus walked the earth many believed that

> *God would deliver the people from their present evils by restoring a king from the descendants of David to rule over Israel. Others thought that the corrupt high priesthood would be replaced with a true one. Others believed that God would raise up two 'anointed' figures, a king and a righteous high priest. Still other people thought that salvation would be brought through a heavenly figure – for example, the angel Michael might defeat the evil angels, or, perhaps, the mysterious, heavenly 'Son of Man' would come in judgment and defeat the enemies of God's people. Still other writers*

114

*say nothing about an agent, anointed or otherwise.*
*They speak of God acting directly in human history.*[133]

It should be clear from this that the disciples would have had no inclination to believe that Jesus was divine or that Jesus was God, even when they admitted that he was the Messiah or the Christ or the Son of God. In their eyes, he was a very special man sent by God to save them from their earthly oppression. Even after his resurrection, they held to this belief as they declared to the risen Jesus, *"But we were hoping that he would be the one to redeem Israel."*[134]

When Jesus told Martha, *"I am the resurrection and the life; whoever believes in me, even if he dies, will live, and everyone who lives and believes in me will never die,"*[135] her response reflected her complete and total misunderstanding of the resurrection that Jesus was proclaiming.

Martha believed that Jesus was describing the restoration of a corpse to life, referring to the resurrection of her brother Lazarus, but Jesus was speaking of a transformation from the physical to the spiritual. Jesus came not to abolish physical death, but rather to transcend it and to raise us to new life in the spirit.

---

[133] Pheme Perkins, *Reading the New Testament: An Introduction*, 3rd Edition, Revised and Updated, Paulist Press, 2012.
[134] Lk 24:21.
[135] Jn 11:25-26.

Jesus delayed his return so as to leave no doubt that Lazarus was truly dead. At the time, it was believed that death could not be proven until three days had elapsed. Lazarus had been dead and in the tomb for four days, which was more than enough time to prove that death had exerted its full power over him and certainly long enough for the body to putrefy and for a stench to rise up.

Jesus delayed his return so that those who were grieving would retain no hope that Lazarus might still remain among the living.

Jesus prolonged his return so that we might come to believe in him and to accept his divinity, for no one but God can exert power over the living and the dead.

Jesus resurrected Lazarus not merely because he could, but to offer into evidence tangible proof of who he was and what was yet to come.

Resurrecting Lazarus foreshadowed not only his own impending death and resurrection, but the resurrection that awaits us all when he comes *again in glory to judge the living and the dead.*[136]

As disciples, we are called to mirror Christ's humanity, to acknowledge his divinity, and above all to follow his command to, *"love the LORD, your God, with all your heart, with all*

---

[136] Nicene Creed.

*your being, with all your strength, and with all your mind, and your neighbor as yourself."*[137]

As a community of believers and as the Body of Christ, we are called to proclaim that Jesus is both the Son of Man and the Son of God.

Ecce homo! *Behold the man!*

Ecce Deus vester! *Behold your God!*

# The Son of Man

We often hear of Jesus that he is the Son of Man and the Son of God, but how often those phrases are heard without truly understanding their meaning. In fact, the phrases are most often understood to mean quite the opposite of their true construct. The "Son of Man" was generally thought to be a

> *heavenly savior figure whose enthronement represents the establishment of God's kingdom. 'Son of Man was not used for Jesus' humanity in contrast to the expression 'Son of God'. For a first-century Jewish audience the phrase 'Son of God' was used in reference to such human figures as the king (Ps 2:7; Isa 9:6), Israel as God's people (Ex 4:22; Hos 11:1), or of persons who were particularly wise or righteous (Wis 2:13, 16).*

---

[137] Lk 10:27.

*Angels may also be referred to as 'sons of God' (Ps 89:7; Dan 3:25).*[138]

Jesus often referred to himself as the Son of Man and while at first blush this may appear to lay claim to his humanity with new understanding of the title, we now can see that rather than denying his deity, he was quite openly proclaiming it. Looking at this with new eyes, we hear his voice in a new and novel way.

When he asks his disciples, *"Who do people say that the Son of Man is? They replied, 'Some say John the Baptist, others Elijah, still others Jeremiah or one of the prophets.' He said to them, 'But who do you say that I am?'"*[139] what do you now hear? How would you respond to Jesus' question, *"But who do you say that I am?"*

Jesus didn't always refer to his divinity quite so obliquely; he didn't just claim to be the Son of Man, in one particular instance, he was even more direct. In response to the question posed by the Jews in the temple:

*Who do you make yourself out to be? Jesus answered, 'If I glorify myself, my glory is worth nothing; but it is my Father who glorifies me, of whom you say, 'He is our God.' You do not know him, but I know him. And if I should say that I do not know him, I would be like you a liar. But I do know him and I keep his word. Abraham*

---

[138] Pheme Perkins, *Reading the New Testament: An Introduction*, 3rd Edition, Revised and Updated, Paulist Press, 2012.
[139] Mt 16:13-15.

*your father rejoiced to see my day; he saw it and was glad. So the Jews said to him, 'You are not yet fifty years old and you have seen Abraham? Jesus said to them, 'Amen, amen, I say to you, before Abraham came to be, I AM.*[140]

It is small wonder that the Jews wished to stone him! He boldly and directly declared himself to be God using the name of God, the name God gave to Moses, אֶהְיֶה אֲשֶׁר אֶהְיֶה, *'ehyeh 'ašer 'ehyeh.*

We can now understand more fully the reaction of the high priest when he asked Jesus if he was the Messiah, the Son of God and he replied, *"From now on you will see 'the Son of Man seated at the right hand of the Power' and 'coming on the clouds of heaven.'"*[141] The high priest asked if Jesus was the Messiah, the anointed one and a king, to whom Jesus responded unequivocally that he was not only the Son of God, a divinely anointed king, but he further proclaimed that he was the Son of Man, that He *was* God.

## How do you see Jesus?

As Christians, we proclaim our belief in Jesus Christ and profess that it is through his passion, death, and resurrection that the gates of heaven have been made available to us. Each of us has a vision, an image of Jesus in our minds, and I would

---

[140] Jn 8:53-58.
[141] Mt 26:64.

suggest that while most are quite similar, if we could project our own personal image of him onto a screen, each would be significantly different.

With the exception of those who lived in Israel and followed Jesus during his brief life here on earth, no one has ever physically laid eyes upon Jesus and therein lies the crux of the matter. There are neither photographs nor paintings available from that time. Jesus never sat for a portrait and cameras were a long time off. The earliest images of Jesus were painted many years, even centuries after his death, resurrection, and ascension into heaven. Not a single painting has ever been created by an artist who *personally* knew the living Jesus or who knew anyone who had personally known him.

So the image you have in your mind of Jesus is just as valid and just as accurate as mine or anyone else's. But, for the moment, let us make a few generalizations concerning the image of Jesus in order to establish some form of baseline for our narrative.

In general we have four normative images of Jesus:

1. as an infant in swaddling clothes lying in a manger;

2. as a healthy and vital young man in his early thirties;

3. as a bloodied and beaten man, carrying or nailed to a wooden cross; and

120

4. as a glorious and glowing vision of God resurrected and ascending into heaven.

Another generalization that we can make is that much of the art of which we are familiar depicts Jesus as a tall, slender, Anglo-Saxon, Caucasian male with kind and loving eyes, a soft and gentle mouth, slender fingers and smooth clean hands sporting a neatly groomed beard and long dark brown hair and impeccably clothed in clean white robes and clean feet shod in neat leather sandals.

All too often we project this image onto his personality while imagining a mild mannered, meek, non-violent, quiet, soft-spoken teacher or preacher. Seldom would we associate words such as strong, outspoken, commanding, demanding, well-educated, revolutionary, or radical with our image of Jesus. We have most assuredly created a wonderful image, and it is a beautiful vision to behold, but it is so far from probative reality that it begs the question of the artists: *"What could they possibly have been thinking?"*

Let us pause for a moment and consider the fact that Jesus *was not* an Anglo-Saxon Caucasian Adonis! He was neither Asian, African, Indian, Polynesian, Hawaiian, Slavic, nor Hispanic. Jesus was a Jew whose ethnicity belongs among the ancient Semitic races that include Akkadians, Phoenicians, Hebrews, and Arabs. As a Jew, Jesus was most likely olive-skinned with dark eyes and, at least by today's measurements, fairly short in stature.

Why is this important? Primarily because our image of Jesus necessarily colors our ability to understand who he truly was and what he taught, and that prevents us from seeing and knowing him to the fullest. Our ability to be his disciple and to truly believe in him will remain circumspect and limited as long as we hold onto an image of a man who is the embodiment of our notion of *human* perfection. This image distracts us from the real Jesus and the radical nature of his presence here on earth.

We must envision Jesus as an everyman, an imperfectly conformed human being, before we can have any hope of divining his *divine* perfection. Jesus was not, despite the musical caricature, a Hollywood superstar nor was he a runway supermodel. As soon as we create such an image in our minds, we lose sight of the authentic Jesus and any ability to discern his voice and his message. We find ourselves struggling to accept freely what complete and honest discipleship demands of us.

# What is a radical?

We can assume, with some reasonable assurance, that virtually everyone no matter their perception, understanding, or knowledge of Jesus, will readily admit that Jesus was much more than just an ordinary or common man.

No matter whether you believe that Jesus was and is God or whether you believe he was a great prophet, a holy man, a revolutionary, or a radical, there can be no doubt that he quite literally changed the world.

But was he really and truly a radical?

The dictionary defines the noun '*radical*' as:

1. a person who holds or follows strong convictions or extreme principles; an extremist; and/or

2. a person who advocates fundamental political, economic, and social reforms by direct and often uncompromising methods.

Those definitions may or may not feel quite correct with any degree of certitude, depending on your own personal convictions and understanding of what a radical might be. Certainly we have all become painfully aware of a wide variety of individuals and groups over the past fifty years or so for whom we would and could easily ascribe the label "*radical*".

Some real life examples with which you may be familiar are:

- Jim Jones, leader of the Peoples Temple, who called his followers to commit mass suicide by drinking poisoned Kool-Aid in 1978;

- The Branch Davidian religious group led by David Koresh, a schismatic sect of the Seventh-day Adventists who died in a fiery assault by federal law enforcement;

- Students for a Democratic Society (SDS) a radical activist movement founded by Tom Hayden, Bill Ayers, Aryeh Neier and Alan Haber in the 1960s;

- The Black Panther Party (BPP) a black revolutionary socialist organization founded by Huey P. Newton and Bobby Seale in the 1960s;

- The Red Army Faction, also known as the Baader-Meinhof Gang, led by Ulrike Meinhof, Andreas Baader, Gudrun Ensslin and Horst Mahler; and

- Al Qaeda, a global Islamic terrorist group led and financed by Osama bin Laden.

A broader more historical list of radical extremism might include:

- 1st – 4th century
  - Pharisees, Jewish Religious leaders
  - Romans and Greeks
- Middle Ages
  - Islam
  - Pagans
  - Catholic Church
- 16th & 17th Centuries
  - Protestant Reformers
- 20th – 21st century
  - Nazism
  - Communism
  - Fundamentalist Christians, sect, and cults
  - Islamic Jihadists

o Racism/Ethnic Cleansing
o Peaceniks, Protesters
o Greenpeace, SDS, PETA

There are many more examples than those previously listed; some more violent and others less so. There have even been a few who have promoted and advocated nonviolent approaches. The unfortunate reality is that we have become far too familiar with radical groups and individuals within our own lifetimes.

Another reality is that, historically, radicals can be found associated within two broad arenas: politics and religion. This may be the rationale behind the meme that you should never discuss politics or religion among family and friends.

Certainly the man that most would place at the top of every list and to whom most would ascribe the label *'radical'* in our time is Osama bin Laden, whose radical Islamic views have promulgated a global pandemic of terror and death with the singular avowed goal of worldwide conversion to and/or annihilation of all who are not followers of his radical version of Islam.

These examples do not in any way form a complete list of radical groups and individuals, and yet there are a few other examples that should be mentioned to provide a more complete expression of what it means to be a radical.

At the opposite of the violence end of the spectrum, we can enumerate the peaceful, non-violent radicals exemplified by such individuals as:

- Mahandas Karamchand Gandhi who, through nonviolent civil disobedience, led India to independence and inspired movements for civil rights and freedom across the world,

- Dr. Martin Luther King, Jr. who led the African-American Civil Rights Movement in the United States using nonviolent civil disobedience based on his Christian beliefs.

It is within the context of this peaceful non-violent genre that we must place Jesus, for he was certainly a radical in his time and place while promoting love toward all and peaceful nonviolent association, even with his enemies.

Recall that Jesus told his disciples, *"You have heard that it was said, 'You shall love your neighbor and hate your enemy.' But I say to you, love your enemies, and pray for those who persecute you, that you may be children of your heavenly Father."*[142]

He also said, *"You have heard that it was said, 'An eye for an eye and a tooth for a tooth.' But I say to you, offer no resistance to one who is evil. When someone strikes you on [your] right cheek, turn the other one to him as well. If anyone wants to go to law with you over*

---

[142] Mt 5:43-45.

*your tunic, hand him your cloak as well. Should anyone press you into service for one mile, go with him for two miles. Give to the one who asks of you, and do not turn your back on one who wants to borrow."*[143]

It is almost as if Jesus took these admonishments and actions straight from either Mahatma Gandhi's or Dr. Martin Luther King's playbook! Of course, we know that it was the complete reverse. Jesus was perhaps the first radical to advocate a peaceful nonviolent approach to human relationships and interactions. So yes, it would appear that we must conclude that Jesus was indeed a radical who called all of us to a revolutionary new way of living, believing, and loving one another.

## What is radical?

The word *'radical'* can also be used as an adjective and the dictionary defines the adjective *'radical'* as:

- of or going to the root or origin; fundamental;

- thoroughgoing or extreme, especially as regards change from accepted or traditional forms;

- favoring drastic political, economic, or social reforms;

---

[143] Mt 5:38-42.

- forming a basis or foundation; or

- existing inherently in a thing or person.

And it is perhaps here that we can uncover and rediscover the radical Jesus. For Jesus, no matter how you may envision him, radically and literally turned the world upside down and forever inalterably changed our relationships with God and our fellow man. He took the world of man that had existed for arguably over five-thousand years and, within a blink of an eye, altered its course, redefining man's relationship with God and reopening the gates of heaven to all who would but follow him.

Fundamentally and quite radically, Jesus altered the Divine relational paradigm that had existed for millennia calling for a new covenant of love, mercy, charity, humility, and forgiveness. No more shall one *"give life for life, eye for eye, tooth for tooth, hand for hand, foot for foot, burn for burn, wound for wound, stripe for stripe"*[144] but, rather, one shall turn the other cheek and forgive the wrongdoer, love one another, give more than is asked, and lend what you have. This was so radical that many found great difficulty in accepting or following his teachings. And surprise, surprise, there are many who still do!

[144] Ex 21:23-25.

128

## View of the Law

Jesus knew the Hebrew Scriptures well and often used them to make a point or to correct misinterpretations of the Law. It is important to remember that he told his disciples *"Do not think that I have come to abolish the law or the prophets. I have come not to abolish but to fulfill. Amen, I say to you, until heaven and earth pass away, not the smallest letter or the smallest part of a letter will pass from the law, until all things have taken place."*[145]

The Pharisees and elders of the Jewish people were in large measure religious zealots, fundamentalists who believed in the strictest interpretation of the Torah or the Law. It was often through their zealotry that Jesus was found not only wanting but in their view a constant offender of the Law. Even something as simple and seemingly unimportant as picking the heads of grain on a Sabbath was contrary to the Law (as *any* level of labor no matter how minute performed on the Sabbath was unlawful). Thus the Pharisees questioned Jesus, *"Look, why are they doing what is unlawful on the Sabbath?"* to which Jesus replied, *"The Sabbath was made for man, not man for the Sabbath. That is why the Son of Man is lord even of the Sabbath."*[146]

Time and again, Jesus would perform some action that affronted the Pharisees' religious sensibilities and say something that appeared to them to be antithetical to the strict interpretation of the Law. Careful review of the Gospels will,

---

[145] Mt 5:17-18.
[146] Mk 2:23-28.

however, clearly expose their hypocritical and tortured misuse of what was written to justify their own actions and beliefs. When he drove out demons they accused him of being the prince of demons;[147] when he cured the man with the withered hand on the Sabbath they conspired to put him to death;[148] when he forgave sins they accused him of blasphemy;[149] and ultimately when he proclaimed that he was the Son of Man, God Incarnate, they crucified him.

## Our relationship with God

His radical ideas concerning man's relationship with God and with one another were often much too difficult a pill to swallow by those who wished to follow him. In Deuteronomy Moses tells the people, *"Hear, O Israel! The LORD is our God, the LORD alone! Therefore, you shall love the LORD, your God, with all your heart, and with all your soul, and with all your strength."*[150] This is a prayer called *Shema Yisrael*, in Hebrew: שְׁמַע יִשְׂרָאֵל, a prayer faithful Jews pray twice a day and which is considered the greatest or first commandment.

When a scholar of the Law (one of the Pharisees) tests Jesus by asking, *"Teacher, which commandment in the law is the greatest,"*[151] Jesus deftly combines the *Shema Yisrael* with a

---

147 Mk 3:22.
148 Mk 3:6.
149 Lk 5:21.
150 Dt 6:4-5.
151 Mt 22:36.

second but significantly related commandment from Leviticus,[152] *"You shall love the LORD your God, with all your heart, with all your soul, and with all your mind. This is the greatest and the first commandment. The second is like it: You shall love your neighbor as yourself. The whole law and the prophets depend on these two commandments."*[153]

This combination radically altered the then accepted Jewish view concerning their relationship with God. Even though Leviticus is one of the books that make up the Pentateuch or the Torah, no one had ever connected the two commandments as tightly together as Jesus had done.

The notion that any relationship between God and man was predicated upon how much one loved their neighbor as well as loving one's self was such a radical idea was nearly incomprehensible. It was a thought that approached blasphemy even to consider that in order to love God one must love self *and* neighbor and that if one failed to love self or others sufficiently, one could not legitimately love God. It was enough to send a fervent Pharisee or Sadducee into religious apoplexy!

## Humility and Service

From the point of view of those who heard him, including his closest friends and disciples, perhaps his most

---

[152] Lv 19:18.
[153] Mt 22:37-40.

radical commandments were the ones that demanded that they humble themselves before God and man. Jesus tells them:

> *The scribes and the Pharisees have taken their seat on the chair of Moses. Therefore, do and observe all things whatsoever they tell you, but do not follow their example. For they preach but they do not practice. They tie up heavy burdens and lay them on people's shoulders, but they will not lift a finger to move them. All their works are performed to be seen. They widen their phylacteries and lengthen their tassels. They love places of honor at banquets, seats of honor in synagogues, greetings in marketplaces, and the salutation 'Rabbi.' As for you, do not be called 'Rabbi.' You have but one teacher, and you are all brothers. Call no one on earth your father; you have but one Father in heaven. Do not be called 'Master;' you have but one master, the Messiah. The greatest among you must be your servant. Whoever exalts himself will be humbled; but whoever humbles himself will be exalted.*[154]

When James and John ask to be seated with Jesus at the place of honor, he tells his disciples,

> *You know that those who are recognized as rulers over the Gentiles lord it over them, and their great ones make their authority over them felt. But it shall not be so among you. Rather, whoever wishes to be great*

---

[154] Mt 23:2-11.

*among you will be your servant; whoever wishes to be first among you will be the slave of all. For the Son of Man did not come to be served but to serve and to give his life as a ransom for many.*[155]

Jesus held no favor for the proud and self-righteous or for those who despised the poor and everyone else. He told the parable of the Pharisee and the tax collector:

*Two people went up to the temple area to pray; one was a Pharisee and the other was a tax collector. The Pharisee took up his position and spoke this prayer to himself, 'O God, I thank you that I am not like the rest of humanity – greedy, dishonest, adulterous – or even like this tax collector. I fast twice a week, and I pay tithes on my whole income.' But the tax collector stood off at a distance and would not even raise his eyes to heaven but beat his breast and prayed, 'O God, be merciful to me a sinner.' I tell you, the latter went home justified, not the former; for everyone who exalts himself will be humbled, and the one who humbles himself will be exalted.*[156]

When an official asked what he must do to inherit eternal life, Jesus told him that beyond obedience to the commandments, *"There is still one thing left for you: sell all that you have and distribute it to the poor, and you will have treasure in*

---

[155] Mk 10:42-44.
[156] Lk 18:10-14.

*heaven. Then come, follow me."*[157] But that was more than the official was willing to do, for he was very attached to all of the earthly riches that he had accumulated.

When Jesus noticed how guests at a banquet were choosing the places of honor at the table, he admonished them by saying:

> *When you are invited by someone to a wedding banquet, do not recline at table in the place of honor. A more distinguished guest than you may have been invited by him, and the host who invited both of you may approach you and say, 'Give your place to this man,' and then you would proceed with embarrassment to take the lowest place. Rather, when you are invited, go and take the lowest place so that when the host comes to you he may say, 'My friend, move up to a higher position.' Then you will enjoy the esteem of your companions at the table. For everyone who exalts himself will be humbled, but the one who humbles himself will be exalted.*[158]

At the Last Supper, Jesus elevated humility and service to others to its highest level when he washed the feet of his disciples.

Imagine how dirty feet would have been in those days, walking or traveling on unpaved streets and roads that were

---

[157] Lk 18:22-23.
[158] Lk 14:8-11.

regularly traversed by horses, sheep, goats, and other animals. Washing feet was considered a duty that only the lowliest of slaves would have to perform. Certainly no master or person of even poor rank would ever stoop so low as to wash the feet of their friends or neighbors.

Yet Jesus did just that and then commanded his disciples to do the same when he told them:

> *You call me 'teacher' and 'master,' and rightly so, for indeed I am. If I, therefore, the master and teacher, have washed your feet, you ought to wash one another's feet. I have given you a model to follow, so that as I have done for you, you should also do. Amen, amen, I say to you no slave is greater than his master nor any messenger greater than the one who sent him. If you understand this, blessed are you if you do it.*[159]

## Jesus was a radical

Read in the context of our new understanding of *radical*, the Gospels portray a very clear picture and a radically new image of Jesus. In the truest sense of the word, Jesus was a *radical* whose *radical* message of faith, hope, and love *radically* confounded the status quo and irrevocably altered history for the better.

---

[159] Jn 13:1-17.

What can be surmised from even the most cursory glance through the Gospels is that every word and action of Jesus was in a very real sense revolutionary and radical. And it must be admitted that whenever radically new ideas are promulgated, and wherever revolutionary actions might occur, not everyone will be prepared to accept or willing to change. Certainly many, if not most of the Jewish religious leaders, were fundamentally opposed to the enormous paradigm shift that arose with the advent of Jesus Christ.

And, despite the rapid expansion of Christianity subsequent to his death and resurrection, widespread opposition to his message has remained for over two-thousand years with no end in sight. The continuing struggle to eliminate even the worst of evils propagated by man – genocide, war, ethnic cleansing, and terrorism – are strong evidence that not everyone has heard or accepted his message.

Yet there is hope, hope that if we can take up the cross of Jesus Christ, that through him, with him, and in him, we can and will radically transform the hearts of all men and promote peace and love for God, neighbor, and ourselves.

# Clothing ourselves in Christ

Jesus was a radical in the truest definition of the word. Not only was his message controversial, but he was constantly and quite publicly moved to call out the religious leaders of the day for their hypocrisy and merciless religious fervor. There were many instances where Jesus responded to their pretentious and elitist beliefs. On one occasion, Jesus spoke to them through a parable describing the kingdom of heaven like a wedding banquet given by a king for his son.[160] Two thoughts come to mind when reading this parable.

The first is that Jesus really didn't like the attitudes of the chief priests and elders very much. Their problem was that they were so hung up on the strict interpretation of the law that they completely missed God's desire for charity and justice. They could not nor would not accept God's invitation to change their lives and to prepare for his banquet.

And the second is that Jesus always enjoyed a good party. Besides attending feasts and meals during his ministry, he often spoke of the kingdom of God as a feast or a banquet.

And in truth a banquet or feast is actually a rather good analogy. The Kingdom of God is like a great party that will be talked about for all eternity because it will go on for all eternity. And the best part is that all are invited, everyone, absolutely everyone. But — and there is always a "but," isn't there — that doesn't mean that anything goes or that all who are invited will be allowed to attend.

While the invitation into the Kingdom is open to everyone, we must prepare ourselves in order to attend the feast. We do this by putting on our *"wedding garment"* or, in

---

[160] Mt 22:1-14.

Saint Paul's words, we put on Christ[161] — we clothe ourselves in love and gentleness — in all that is worthy of the Kingdom. We need to prepare ourselves, not because we must, but because we know we are entering into the presence of a loving, gracious, and forgiving God.

When we are Christian in name only or when we adopt a stance we call Christian that overlooks justice and hospitality toward others, we are depriving the world of Christ's influence through us. We are also depriving ourselves of the opportunity to change our own lives. A culture of cynicism and emphasis on form rather than substance encourages a weak response rather than a strong commitment.

Jesus did not make light of people and their concerns, but both ultimately and on a daily basis poured out his life as he listened, healed, taught and loved both his friends and strangers. God created us with equal dignity and He expects us to treat others in the same way. How we respond to His expectations measures the quality of our faith.

What is our attitude when we say each Sunday in the Creed: "*I look for the resurrection of the dead and the life of the world to come*"[162]? We are called to believe this with all our heart, but do we really do so? Are we not often strongly attached to the things of this world, perhaps even to the point of partially denying our faith? Think of the guests in the parable. Each had

---

[161] Gal 3:27.
[162] Nicene Creed.

an excuse for not attending and all were held back by some worldly reason that kept them from the kingdom of heaven. Each Sunday we proclaim our faith in Christ but do we really long for him with all our heart?

As God calls us all to Himself, He gives us the power to respond. That power is the faith to trust in God and assent to His truth. In this sense *"faith is a gift from God, a supernatural virtue infused by him"*. Faith is grace. In other words, we can describe faith as God's love reaching out to us and His love in us reaching back to Him. Without God's initiative of love, we could not know God or have a relationship with Him.

As love is freely given, it is freely received. As a free acceptance of God's love, faith is truly a human act, for God does not impose love on us. Faith is a supremely free act that God gives us. He reaches out to us with love and his love carries us back to him. God calls us all with his love. His chosen are those of us who freely say "Yes" and faith is our simple "Yes" to that love. While God's love might seem faint or absent at times, He still points us toward our ultimate destination: life eternal with Him. Faith is our road to eternal life.

The Feast that God prepares for us is like a test that is set before us: we must believe that the Feast is true, we must hope for this Feast as the single motive of all our desires, and we must love this Feast as that which will give us the food we most need to nourish both our soul and our body. We must, above all, show that we are worthy of being admitted to this Feast through total faith and confidence in God.

Jesus affirms the boundless generosity and inclusive reach of God's grace, but he also tells us that for us to be worthy of God's gift requires nothing less than for us to give our whole life to the glory of God.

# What did Jesus do?

Too often, as Christians, we take our faith for granted, never questioning what we believe and never attempting to gain greater understanding of what it is that we profess. It is as if at some point in our lives we have placed ourselves on autopilot expecting God to steer the course while we sit back, relax and enjoy the ride. When asked to attend to the simplest of tasks or read the briefest of instructions, we continue to dwell within ourselves and take a pass on discovering the deeper meaning that lies before us.

How many times have we presented ourselves before God and offered ourselves and our prayers in praise and thanksgiving while allowing our minds to drift far beyond the walls of God's house? How many times have we left the church with no memory retained of what was prayed or what was read or even what was spoken? We remember entering and we remember leaving, but nothing in between. It is as if we came, we sat, we took a nap, we rose, we turned, and then we left – weekly obligation fulfilled.

A complete stranger recently asked in all seriousness, *"What did Jesus do for three days in hell?"* obviously referring to the statement found in the Apostles Creed where we pray, *"was crucified, died and was buried; he descended into hell; on the third day he rose again from the dead; ..."* I later recounted this question and my response to a small faith-sharing group and was surprised that no one in attendance knew quite how to respond to the question.

While the Apostles Creed uses the word *hell* to describe where Jesus went after his death, the Hebrew word was *sheol*. Unlike our current belief of *hell* as the place of the damned, ancient Jewish belief was that *sheol* in a very general way designated the kingdom of the dead, which included both the good as well as the bad.

Jesus came to save all of mankind, both the living *and* the dead, which includes all those who came before, all who were living then, as well as all those who would come after. Thus, after his death, Jesus descended into the netherworld, the kingdom of the dead, *sheol* or *hell*, to lead the good who had died before him into paradise.

How many times have we recited the Apostles Creed and declared that Jesus descended into hell without ever asking why or without ever asking what did he do for those three days in hell? How often have our lips moved and our voices sounded the words in prayer while our minds and hearts are absent from that time and place, lost in another dimension of thought and awareness?

Perhaps it is time to open our hearts and minds to the presence of God in our lives and to refocus our attention and energy on our relationship with Him who created us and loves us beyond all measure. Perhaps it is time to delve deeper into what it is that we pray, what it is that we read, and what it is that God is saying to each of us. Perhaps it is time for us to wake up and realize that the autopilot we have been relying on may not be taking us where we wish to go.

## To know that He is God

Jesus invites three of his closest friends to hike with him up a mountain where he is transfigured before them.[163] It is clear from the reading that the apostles did not have a clue as to what was happening, and I suspect many of us might fall into that very same category.

Transfiguration is not an easy word to grasp. Outside of the Bible, the only recent use that I can recall is in the Harry Potter books by J.K. Rowling where the young wizards attend a "Transfiguration" class. But the class really isn't about transfiguration but rather transformation, which is defined as changing from one thing into another, such as from a human into a dog or a cat. Jesus was transfigured rather than

---

[163] Mk 9:2-8.

transformed and, in this case, transfiguration allows the three Apostles to see the truth of Jesus as the only Son of God. Jesus does not change form. He remains himself; it is his divinity that is revealed.

Transfiguration is defined as a marked change in form or appearance; a metamorphosis. In school long ago, I remember being taught that you cannot define a word using the word itself. For example, you cannot define *transfiguration* as the act of being transfigured. That makes perfect sense to me. But I believe that you should also never use obscure and unfamiliar words within a definition, words such as *metamorphosis*. The definition of *metamorphosis* is a change of physical form, structure, or substance especially by supernatural means. And *supernatural* is defined as departing from what is usual or normal, especially so as to appear to transcend the laws of nature. So, if we really think about it, transfiguration simply means to change one's physical appearance in some unknown or abnormal way.

At the beginning of his masterpiece The Lord of the Rings, J.R.R. Tolkien introduces one of his main characters, the wizard Gandalf the Grey. Later, after battling the Balrog for many days, Gandalf dies, only to be reborn, to be transfigured as Gandalf the White.[164]

------

[164] J.R.R. Tolkien, The Lord of the Rings, Vol. I, The Fellowship of the Rings, 1954.

Mark does not describe the transfiguration of Jesus other than to say, *"He was transfigured before them and his clothes became dazzling white..."*[165] We can only imagine to what extent his physical appearance was changed.

We are reminded at various times throughout the Bible that no one can see the face of God and live. God is often described as a light so bright as to overwhelm our human senses. This causes us to pause and try to find some means of comprehending and imagining the glory of God. Like the three blind men who are confronted with an elephant (a thing that they have never before encountered), we grope blindly in order to come to conclusions beyond reason or fact.

How many of us have stood on the shores of a lake, such as beautiful Lake Tahoe or a great sea or an ocean, watching the waves while admiring the beauty and vastness of the waters and observed how wonderful a sight it was to behold. Yet beneath the surface is a world far more beautiful, more wondrous, more enchanting than one could ever imagine.

As a scuba diver, I have had the opportunity to dive in many places around the world, and yet I am always amazed at the hidden treasures that lie just beneath the surface: the abundance and variety of sea life, the vivid colors, the quiet stillness, the ever changing dynamics of a world unknown and unseen by those who have never looked below the surface. I believe that in a small way, when we consider the hidden

---

[165] Mk 9:2-3.

beauty that surrounds us, we can begin to understand the awesome power, glory, and beauty that is God.

St. Ephraim was a 4th century Syrian and an ordained deacon in Mesopotamia (now Turkey.) Recognized as a doctor of the Church, he was renowned as the lyre or harp of the Holy Spirit. He explained the Transfiguration of Jesus quite clearly and with great understanding.

He taught that to discover why Jesus was transfigured, we must first see Jesus through the eyes of his apostles. To the apostles, Jesus was just a man, the son of Mary and Joseph. They saw Jesus as a normal human being, eating and drinking, working and sweating, growing tired and falling asleep. They had no idea that Jesus was God.

In order for the apostles to comprehend his true nature, Jesus took them up the mountain and was transfigured before their eyes. They heard the voice of God and they saw with their own eyes Jesus transfigured. Through this transfiguration, they came to believe that Jesus was divine and that he truly was the Son of God.

But why did Jesus feel it necessary to reveal his divinity? St. Ephraim further explains that He revealed his divinity, his mighty power, and his divine glory to prepare the apostles for what was yet to come, and to help them understand the true nature of his impending passion, death, and resurrection. Jesus revealed his divine nature so that the apostles, and all who would follow him, could understand that it was not for any lack of power on his part that he allowed himself to be crucified by his enemies, but rather because he had freely chosen to suffer in that way for our salvation.

Looking out above the surface of the sea, we cannot hope to grasp the richness of what lies beneath the waves. We are blind to the fullness of life that exists beyond our senses. Jesus was transfigured before his friends so that they could, and we can, if only for a moment, see beyond the surface, to see the beauty of his reality, to know that he was more than just a man, and to know that he is God.

# Chapter Seven

## We are the body of Christ

*For all of you who were baptized into Christ*
*have clothed yourselves with Christ.*
*There is neither Jew nor Greek,*
*there is neither slave nor free person,*

*There is not male and female;*
*for you are all one in Christ Jesus.*

Gal 3:27-28

After His resurrection, Jesus called all of His disciples to proclaim the Good News to all people throughout the world. He gave Peter the keys to the Kingdom and placed him at the head of the church, the body of Christ. Through the apostles and early Church fathers, God has continued to speak to all who would listen.

# One flock, One Shepherd

I frequently remind my religious education students that God loves us no matter what happens in our lives. It makes no difference whether we want it, whether we ask for it, or whether we believe that we deserve it, He still loves us. We are His children. He created us in his image.

Meister Eckhart once spoke of God's love, *"He yearns after us, and in the depth of His Divine Being waves of longing break forth, to reveal to us the abyss of His Godhead, and the fullness of His essence; He hastens to identify Himself with us...God loveth men not less than He loveth Himself. If thou really lovest thyself, thou lovest all men as thyself; as long as thou lovest any one less than thyself, thou dost not really love thyself. That man is right who loves all men as himself."* [166]

True love does not come from within us. It comes from God. You cannot know love through the external. It cannot be

---

[166] Justs Junkulis, *10 Jewels of Christian Mysticism: A Selection of Western Tradition Primary Texts*, "Meister Eckhart's Sermons" by Johannes Eckhart, Sermon IV, True Hearing, 2013.

found in a book or a lecture. It must be experienced by living and loving God. We live in a world that has little time for God and, as a consequence, little time for love. It is because we know so little of God that we fail to find true love.

I further remind my students that we owe God our love in return. He created us out of love and you have to love Him for our creation. Up to this point, all heads are usually nodding in agreement. But then comes the kicker. Since God created us out of love, we must love Him in return. We must also love God's creation, all of it, and most importantly every person created by God. If you don't love all that He has created, then how can you truly love God?

Loving others is seldom easy, and it often comes with a heavy price. Certainly God paid dearly with the death of His only Son on the cross, so we must expect to pay the price when we love God and love others. We may face rejection and abuse and perhaps even suffering or death, but if you love God, you have no choice but to love your neighbor as yourself.

God's love for us is manifested through Jesus who died so that we could know God's love. God so loved the world that He sent His only son, Jesus Christ, who became man, suffered, died, and rose for the forgiveness of sin and the salvation of the whole world. Everyone is included, no exceptions. God loves all of us, even those who might not believe in Him. Jesus said, *"I have other sheep that do not belong to this fold. These also I must lead, and they will hear my voice, and there will be one flock, one shepherd.*"[167] God runs an *"all inclusive"* club where everyone is invited and welcome to join.

Jesus tells us, *"I am the good shepherd."*[168] References to shepherds can be found throughout the Bible. Kings and those in political and religious leadership positions are often metaphorically spoken of as shepherds of their people. It is a reference that is generally understood and accepted, although today most of us would respond negatively if we were to be called sheep. We think of sheep as timid creatures that are not very bright; creatures easily fooled by wolves in sheep's clothing or creatures that can be led like lambs to the slaughter. The imagery is just not very appealing, to say the least.

But in the English language, sheep have a rather unique distinction because the same word is used for both the singular and the plural. Sheep belong to a flock that follows a shepherd whom they trust to keep them safe. The shepherd knows his flock and, as Jesus tells us, *"I am the good shepherd, and I know mine and mine know me, just as the Father knows me and I know the Father; and I will lay down my life for the sheep."*[169] To be a Christian means we belong to Christ who is the good shepherd, and it means we belong together, not as individuals, but as a community of believers who share in the body of Christ and our love for one another.

---

[167] Jn 10:16.
[168] Jn 10:11.
[169] Jn 10:14-15.

But ... does that have to include everyone — even those who aren't, you know, like us? After all, if they aren't with us, they must be against us. Right? How can they be included when they don't believe everything that we believe? If they aren't part of our community of believers then they can't be loved by God quite as much as we are. Can they? The truth is that it is not up to us to decide who is in or who is out. The Good Shepherd loves all and leads all, not just our flock.

But if everyone is invited, who will be included? Jesus tells us, "*For I was hungry and you gave me food, I was thirsty and you gave me drink, a stranger and you welcomed me, naked and you clothed me, ill and you cared for me, in prison and you visited me.*"[170]

So what are we to do? For starters, like Jesus, we must open our hearts and arms to everyone. We must love our neighbor as our self. We must love everyone as our Heavenly Father loves each of us. For if we love the stranger, we will soon discover that the stranger is no longer strange but rather our brother or sister.

When we look at others through the eyes of Christ, we will see as in a mirror a reflection of our self — the image and likeness of God.

---

[170] Mt 25:35-36.

# We Belong to God

*"The greatest among you must be your servant. Whoever exalts himself will be humbled; but whoever humbles himself will be exalted."*[171]

Like the Scribes and Pharisees, we often place ourselves on a pedestal believing that we have special gifts or talents that make us superior to others while we conveniently forget that we all have our shortcomings and weaknesses. Or at least we wish to forget, so that we don't have to acknowledge to others that we are not quite as good as we might have them believe. For some the statement, *"Oh Lord, it's hard to be humble, when you're perfect in every way,"*[172] feels so right and true, but in truth there is only one who has the right to make that statement, and He died for us on a cross some two-thousand years ago.

The word 'humility' comes from the Latin word 'humus,' which means soil and is generally associated with words such as abject, ignoble, of poor condition, or not worth much. More often than not, we perceive a humble person as meek, stooped over with downcast eyes and a soft, timid voice, trying very hard never to be noticed or recognized. However, this is not the vision offered by Jesus. Rather, his is one of a strong sense of self that begins in humility; we are in this together and we need

---

[171] Mt 23:11-12.
[172] Mac Davis, *It's Hard To Be Humble,* 1980.

and depend on one another, and we must use our gifts for the good of others and the glory of God.

Saint Thomas Aquinas wrote that *"The virtue of humility consists in keeping oneself within one's own bounds, not reaching out to things above one, but submitting to one's superior."*[173] And Saint Augustine said that God accepts sacrifices only from the altar of humility. We humble ourselves by being ourselves and God exalts us for who we are.

Humility is a gift neither earned nor self-created. When we live courageously in the spirit of communion with others, we open ourselves to seeing others through God's eyes and from His perspective. Humility begins with the knowledge that we belong to God. It is the sense that all of God's creation is important, and that our existence depends on our relationship with others. It is not a matter of denying our own self-interest but in seeing how our interests are connected to the well-being of others.

Humility does not call for us to reject or disparage our God given gifts, nor does it require us to think of our gifts as less valued than the gifts God has given others. God has entrusted each of us with certain gifts and abilities, and He expects that we use those gifts to their fullest. God measures each of us on our own merit. It is not a competition. What others achieve is never part of the equation because before God everyone stands alone.

---

[173] Saint Thomas Aquinas, *Summa contra Gentiles, Bk IV, Ch. IV,* 1264.

As I reflect upon what Jesus teaches us concerning the greatest and the least, I can't help but be reminded of my parents, for they were true examples of humility and holiness.

They were both born in the mid-1920s in northeast Missouri and grew up on farms during the depression era. Dad served as a Navy corpsman attached to the Marine Corps in the South Pacific during World War II. He came home after the war and married mom a day after her 21st birthday.

My mother graduated from high school after 2-1/2 years and attended college for only one year. She read voraciously and even taught school for a short while. She eventually became an award-winning journalist while working at home and raising eleven children.

Dad, with a silly grin on his face, always bragged that he graduated from high-school fourth in his class while casually neglecting to mention that there were only four in his class. But what he could do with his hands was a wonder to behold. He built a walnut china hutch as a wedding present for one of my brothers … starting from the tree.

They never put on airs or pretended to be anyone but themselves. God was always present in our lives. Everyone was always welcome in our home for the doors were never locked. And there was always room for more at the table.

When they were killed in a traffic accident, the wake and funeral were attended by more people than our small town of two-thousand could accommodate. Their lives and their actions had touched so many through their simple acts of kindness and generosity, even to some whom they had never even met. They gave of themselves freely while never asking or expecting anything in return, and what they gave was always their very, very best.

My parents taught us that we do not live alone, that we can be proud of who we are, while never believing that we are entitled or superior to others. They taught us that the world will become a better place when we freely offer our God given gifts to others, and that every gift offered is returned and magnified many times by the grace and gifts of others.

Saint Paul in writing to the Romans said, "… *I tell everyone among you not to think of himself more highly than one ought to think, but to think soberly, each according to the measure of faith that God has apportioned. For as in one body we have many parts, and all the parts do not have the same function, so we, though many, are one body in Christ and individually parts of one another.*"[174]

Jesus tells us that becoming a servant, a child, a humble person are ways of revealing true godliness. Holiness requires us to discard anything that hides God's goodness within us.

As human beings, we all wish to stand out and to be recognized as unique and valued members of society, but we occasionally need to step down from our pedestals and learn to

---

[174] Rm 12:3-4.

become servants of God. If we are willing to put our pride aside, our hearts will be filled to overflowing with God's grace and love.

As Blessed Mother Teresa, who was herself a model of great humility, once said, *"We can do no great things, only small things with great love."* [175]

# The choice is ours

Meister Eckhart wrote that "*God loved us when we were not, and when we were His foes ... Whether we go near or far, God never goes far away but always stands nearby; and even if He cannot remain within, He never goes further than outside the door.*" [176]

What a statement of love. Who else but God would stick around no matter how we might treat Him. Saint Augustine wrote that "*God loves each one of us as if there were only one of us to love.*" [177] Saint John wrote, "*In this is love, not that we loved God but that God loved us.*" [178] "*We love because God first loved us.*" [179]

We are free to choose whom and what we love. We can love the darkness of sin or we can love the light of God's

---

[175] One of the most often repeated quotes attributed to Blessed Mother Teresa of Calcutta.

[176] Meister Eckhard, The Kingdom of Heaven with You – Volume I, translated by C. M. Vega.

[177] Attributed to Saint Augustine, source unknown.

[178] 1 Jn 4:10.

[179] 1 Jn 4:19.

unconditional love which is the source of all joy. We are free to choose.

God is the source and giver of all that is good. We have received and continue to receive so many gifts from Him and yet we often forget or ignore His magnificent gifts. St. Paul tells us that "...*by grace you have been saved through faith, and this is not from you; it is the gift of God.*"[180] And the ultimate gift of all, we hear in the Gospel, "*For God so loved the world that He gave his only Son, so that everyone who believes in him might not perish but might have eternal life.*"[181]

How often have we asked God for something: a new house, a happy family, a comfortable life, a baby, reconciliation with a friend, healing from a long ailment, or more? We cross our fingers and hope that God in His time will grant our dreams. But sometimes because we have to wait for weeks, months, or even years, we begin to doubt God. We become impatient, wanting an instant answer or solution instead of waiting. In our desire to speed up the process, we end up making hasty decisions that lead us to sin or to commit mistakes.

Most of our sins are caused by our impatience and unwillingness to deal with uncertainty and suffering. We want resolution without delay or pain. When the devil sees this growing impatience in us, he will offer an "*instant solution*" – a

---

[180] Eph 2:8.
[181] Jn 3:16.

very tempting alternative to God's promise. This modern poisonous snake bites when one becomes impatient.

But God's love and forgiveness never cease. Anyone who looks and believes in him will be saved.[182] But believing means going beyond words, it means following in the footsteps of Jesus. The crucifix symbolizes Jesus' patience and endurance; to hold on until death. It should give us the strength to move on and carry our daily crosses with determination and faith.

So in our present world of quick fixes, rush jobs, instant food, digital downloads, internet, cut and paste, overnight affairs, and divorce, let us slow down and cultivate more patience. Let us pause, watch a sunset, spend time with a loved one, or visit the Blessed Sacrament for an hour. To be patient is to be calm, to allow God to be in control, to smile when plans are not working well, to gracefully tolerate delays, to embrace the unknown, and to be hopeful. The joy in discovering the simple things of life can teach us the virtue of patience. Open our eyes. Good things are fruits of hard work, patience, and endurance.

Jesus tries to tell Nicodemus that everyone who believes in him will enjoy eternal life, and that those who know who they are in the light of Christ will more clearly desire their identities to be shown in the works of *"light"* which they live.[183] The converse is true as well. If we do not know or refuse to

---

[182] Jn 3:14.
[183] Jn 3:14-21.

accept who we are, then that personal darkness will play hide and seek with our lives. We will seek to hide in the darkness and secretly hope our selfishness might never be exposed.

In a splendid passage from Ephesians, Saint Paul is well aware of our reluctance to entrust ourselves to God's love. That is why he seems compelled to reiterate: *"I repeat, it is owing to God's favor that salvation is yours through faith. This is not your own doing. It is God's gift. Neither is it a reward for anything you have accomplished."*[184]

Paul reiterates this teaching about divine love in his letter to the Ephesians. He declares that God saves us through Christ. But why should God do this? It is certainly not because we desire it. In fact, Paul claims that God saved us while we were still in our transgressions, mired in our sinfulness. God saves us out of mercy — that covenantal characteristic known in the Hebrew tradition as loving-kindness or steadfast love. God's merciful love alone marks the *"ends of being and ideal grace."*[185]

However — and it is a significant however — God does not force anything upon us. We are free to choose. We can accept God's loving gestures or we can refuse them. Before the Israelites could return to the Promised Land from their bondage and slavery in Babylon, they had to choose to return to God.[186] Jesus tells Nicodemus that all people can choose to believe or

---

[184] Eph 2:8-9.
[185] Elizabeth Barret Browning, *Sonnet 43, How Do I Love Thee?*
[186] 1 Chr 3614-21.

not believe in him, but that they can and too often do prefer the darkness to the light *"because their works were evil."*[187] There has always been a choice. Today the choice is ours to make, but will we make it?

# The temple of God

When asked for a sign of his authority, Jesus told the Jews that if they destroyed the temple, he would raise it up in three days.[188] The Jews, of course, did not understand what Jesus meant. Like many of us, they tended to interpret things far too literally.

We have this notion of temples or churches as places where God resides. We forget that God is everywhere. Churches are buildings built by man for our own purposes, not for God's. A church is a place where we can go to feel closer to God, to worship, and to pray together to our Creator.

Saint Augustine wrote that *"God's temple is holy," and you are that temple: all you who believe in Christ and whose belief makes you love him. All who believe in this way are like the living stones which go to build God's temple, and like the rot-proof timber used in the framework of the ark which the flood waters could not submerge. It*

---

[187] Jn 3:1-20.
[188] Jn 2:18-19.

*is in this temple, that is, in ourselves, that prayer is addressed to God and heard by Him."*[189]

Saint Paul tells us that we are members of Christ's body and, therefore, we are individually and collectively temples of God. He wrote, "*Do you not know that your body is a temple of the Holy Spirit within you, whom you have from God, and that you are not your own?*"[190]

Johannes Tauler, a 14th century Dominican and disciple of Meister Eckhart, similarly wrote that *"Our Lord Jesus Christ, the Eternal Son of God has faithfully taught us here, what we must do that our hearts may be clean and pure houses of prayer; for man is really and truly a Holy Temple of God."*[191]

In order for us to worship and give praise and thanks to God as we should, we must love and respect others. We cannot love God if we do not love all that He has created. True and honest worship demands that we love and respect those whom He has created in His own image and likeness.

When a scholar of the law asked Jesus:

*Teacher, which commandment in the law is the greatest? He said to him, "You shall love the LORD, your God, with all your heart, with all your soul, and*

---

[189] Saint Augustine, *City of God*. Translation by Gerald G. Walsh, S.J. 1958.
[190] 1 Cor 19.
[191] Justs Junkulis, *10 Jewels of Christian Mysticism: A Selection of Western Tradition Primary Texts*, "The Inner Way" by Johannes Tauler, Sermon XXXVI, At the dedication of a church. The Second Sermon", 2013.

*with all your mind. This is the greatest and the first commandment. The second is like it: You shall love your neighbor as yourself. The whole law and the prophets depend on these two commandments.*[192]

We must recognize that when we hurt others, we are desecrating the temple of the Holy Spirit. We are in a very real sense behaving exactly like those vendors and moneychangers whom Jesus drove from the temple.[193] When we fail to live by the Ten Commandments, when we lie, steal, or covet what others might have, when we lash out in anger, criticizing people or causing them pain, we are desecrating their and our temples, their and our places of worship, and God's holy sanctuary.

Loving God means loving all that God has created because He created all out of love. Underlying one of my student's incredulousness when he asked whether he was required to love even cops, was an important and fundamental fact. While we, as children of God who have been created in His image and likeness, must love all that God has created, we are not required to *like* everyone. God created each of us out of love but not all return his love by following His commandments. We are not asked to love evil, to condone or support those who may do us harm, to promote hatred, bigotry, or violence. But just as God loves everyone no matter what they have done or may do, so must we as well.

---

[192] Mt 22:36-40.
[193] Mt 21:12-13, Mk 11:15-17, Lk 19:45-46, Jn 2:14-16.

I believe that Jesus gave us the words and showed us by his example how we must love others when at his crucifixion he prayed to God and said, *"Father, forgive them, they know not what they do."*[194]

It is of utmost importance that we recognize that we are all the body of Christ, the ever living temple of the Holy Spirit. Let us join together in love to worship God who created each of us in love, with love, and for love.

## Love one another

Jerome Murphy-O'Connor wrote in The First Letter to the Corinthians in the New Jerome Biblical Commentary that

> *A Eucharistic community cannot be a true gathering in which there are the 'haves' and the 'have nots.' In other words, Paul...clearly states that a Jesus community itself is the necessary basis for any and every celebration of the Eucharist, not vice versa. A genuine Eucharist cannot involve only a few people who communally celebrate the Eucharistic meal while the majority are present basically as onlookers. The essence of his [Paul's] reaction is that there can be no Eucharist*

---

[194] Lk 23:34.

*in a community whose members do not love one another.*[195]

Saint Paul himself writes of the absolute importance of love, telling us that if one does not have love, then one has nothing, for love is the greatest gift one can give to another. What should be emphasized here is that Saint Paul is speaking of a specific type of love. The word *agápē* is one of the four words for love found in Koine Greek. The first is *storge*, which is brotherly love; the second is *philia*, which is the love between friends; the third is *eros*, which is romantic love or the sense of "being in love"; and the fourth type of love is *agápē*, which is the love that God has for us and that we have for God.

As God's creation, we have been created in His image and likeness and are bound to love all of His creation just as we love our Creator. That means that *agápē* extends to the love of one another without condition or measure. And that is a very difficult thing to accept and even more to accomplish.

Jesus tells us, *"This is my commandment: love one another as I love you. No one has greater love than this, to lay down one's life for one's friends."*[196] This is *agápē*. Jesus neither equivocates nor does he offer conditions upon which we can love one but not another. He clearly and succinctly commands us to *"love one another."* No ifs, ands, or buts.

---

[195] Jerome Murphy-O'Connor, *New Jerome Biblical Commentary: The First Letter to the Corinthians*, 1990.
[196] Jn 15:1-13.

Jesus gave us the Eucharist, the purest offering of his body and blood, as a real and substantive expression of his love for us, and it is his gift of *agápe* which we receive every time we celebrate the Eucharist. For this reason, Saint Paul tells us that in order to receive the *agápe* of our Lord and Savior, we must love one another. We must exemplify and extend *agápe* to all of our brothers and sisters. To the extent that we limit ourselves in love for one another, we diminish our love for Jesus.

Dorothy Day once said, *"I really only love God as much as I love the person I love the least."*[197] Perhaps we should consider how much we love or fail to love others as a direct measure of our love for God. It is certainly something to think about.

# Overflowing with God

There is a certain ecstasy that emanates from within and shines forth with a radiance so bright it overwhelms every sensation, a joy that cannot be contained nor suppressed, and a beauty that surprises all who are witness to a soul filled to overflowing with Almighty God. Perhaps it is for no other reason than that such experiences are truly rare, but I believe it is because we steadfastly refuse to open ourselves to observing those breath-taking moments should they flash before our eyes. We seldom place ourselves on the pathway that leads to such moments, and even if we should do so, we find our eyes closed or we are facing in the wrong direction.

---

[197] Dorothy Day, Statement attributed to her, no published source known.

It is a malady that we find woven throughout the fabric of human history, that strange ailment that finds us staring into the sun to see the light, only to be blinded by its brightness. Perhaps we can come to understand such moments by recalling the times when even those closest to Jesus failed to recognize him, such as when Mary of Magdala stood face-to-face with Jesus at the empty tomb, yet she thought he was the gardener,[198] or when the two disciples did not recognize him on the road to Emmaus until he broke bread with them.[199]

A soul that is filled completely with God shines brighter than the sun or the most brilliant star. There is an essence that surrounds and somehow illuminates even the darkest corner. To come in contact with such a moment leaves no doubt that God has granted you a taste of heaven and a glimpse into His coming glory.

I believe with all my heart that I have been blessed a handful of times in my life to have experienced such moments, and each has served to increase my faith and to fill me with a hunger for more. But it has also opened my eyes to see God in anyone and everyone that I may encounter.

My visits with my friend Father John and my cousin's husband Wes were two such moments. God filled them. I saw Him in their eyes, I heard Him in their voices, and I felt Him through their touch.

---

[198] Jn 20:15.
[199] Lk 24:31.

At his Confirmation, a young man whom I had prepared for the sacrament was another such experience. I saw an at-risk student whose young life was filled with disturbing events which included an unknown father, maternal abandonment, juvenile delinquency, and gang association, literally transfigured before me. God filled him completely and I caught a glimpse of His glory.

Perhaps the most poignant and moving moment occurred during one Easter Vigil celebration as I observed a small group of elect receive the sacraments of Baptism, Confirmation, and Eucharist. The joy on each face was evident, but was so much more visible on the face of one eighth grade girl, a young teenager who quite literally was overflowing with the presence of God.

As she wiped her hair with a towel after her baptism, tears of pure ecstasy poured from her eyes and her radiant smile filled the space with a near beatific vision of loveliness. Full of God's love, she only increased in angelic radiance as she received the Holy Spirit and the Body and Blood of our Lord Jesus Christ. There could be no doubt that all who were in her presence shared a brief taste of heaven and a glimpse of His glory.

Some theologians and biblical scholars are convinced that those closest to Jesus, his personal friends and disciples, believed that he was a prophet and a holy man, but did not believe that he was divine. And perhaps they are correct in their convictions but, being God, Jesus was by his very nature filled completely with God, by God, and of God and that could never have been hidden from them.

It is impossible to place the light that is God in darkness. Darkness is nothing but the absence of light, and light by its very essence, destroys the darkness. Jesus is the light that *"shines in the darkness, and the darkness has not overcome it."*[200]

## Love and fear

Fear and love are mutually exclusive. There can be no fear in love for fear exists only in the darkness and the unknowing. Love can only exist where there is no fear because love only lives in the light of truth and understanding.

*We have come to know and to believe in the love God has for us. God is love, and whoever remains in love remains in God and God in him. There is no fear in love, but perfect love drives out fear because fear has to do with punishment, and so one who fears is not yet perfect in love. We love because He first loved us. If anyone says, 'I love God,' but hates his brother, he is a liar; for whoever does not love a brother whom he has seen cannot love God whom he has not seen. This is the*

---

[200] Jn 1:5.

*commandment we have from him: Whoever loves God must also love his brother.*[201]

Jesus asked his disciples, *"Who are my brothers?"* and told his disciples, *"whoever does the will of my heavenly Father is my brother, and sister, and mother."*[202] We are the one body of Christ who live in a community of brothers and sisters who belong to our Lord Jesus Christ. Through baptism, we become a new creation and an indivisible and integral part of the community.

Jerome Murphy-O'Connor believes that St. Paul moved beyond the normal idea of community to a far more radical one:

*We think of individuals coming together to create community. For Paul it is precisely the reverse. The community is a radically new reality (1 Cor 1:28) which makes the believer a new creation (2 Cor 5:17). We consider unity as something to be created, whereas Paul saw this unity as primary and envisaged individuals as being changed by absorption into the unity.*[203]

We are called by Jesus to love our brothers and sisters, to embrace each other as family, and to become a gospel community. But we should ask ourselves this question as Jesus did, *"Who are our brothers and sisters?"*

--------

[201] 1 Jn 4:16, 18-21.

[202] Mt 12:48-50.

[203] Jerome Murphy-O'Connor, *Keys to First Corinthians: Revisiting the Major Issues*, 2009.

Are they those who join with us at Eucharist each weekend? Are they the only ones who we call our brothers and sisters? Or are there others who also belong to the body of Christ but who remain unseen and apart from our community?

An essential element of a community is found in its spelling: *com* is derived from the Latin word *cum* which means *with* or *together* and the last five letters – *unity* – define its essence. We are all one in Christ Jesus, united in our love of God and love of our neighbor. We are called to seek out that which we have lost, just as Jesus taught us with the parables of the lost sheep, the lost coin, and the lost son.[204] Let us pray for those whom we do not find among us, and let us rejoice and welcome them back into our midst.

---

[204] Lk 15.

# Part III

Knock, and the door will open

# I do believe

*I listen for your voice but seldom hear it,*
*for I do not hear your silence.*
*I look but do not find you,*
*for I do not see you near me.*
*I reach for you to guide me, but stumble*
*for I do not feel you holding me,*
*I weep in all my loneliness,*
*for I forget you're always with me,*
*I forget that you are there for me,*
*and for that I am so ashamed.*
*I ask you to forgive me,*
*I do believe, help me in my unbelief.*

# Chapter Eight

## Our hearts were burning

*And it happened that,*
*while he was with them at table,*
*he took bread, said the blessing,*
*broke it, and gave it to them.*
*With that their eyes were opened*
*and they recognized him,*
*but he vanished from their sight.*

*Then they said to each other,*
*"Were not our hearts burning within us*
*while he spoke to us on the way*
*and opened the scriptures to us?"*

Luke 24:30-32

# Do you like it?

Have you ever wondered why God gave us such wondrous beauty, beauty that goes far beyond even our most basic needs? As Max Lucado asks, *"Did He have to give the birds a song and the mountains a peak? Was He required to put stripes on the zebra and the hump on the camel? Why wrap creation in such splendor? Why go to such trouble to give such gifts?"*[205] If you think about it, there really is no compelling reason for such wonders other than God's desire to create everything out of His love.

We are all familiar with the idea of God's love. We have certainly heard it often enough and in so many ways how God loves us unconditionally, completely, fully, and beyond measure. We have heard that He sent His only Son into this world to become one of us and to suffer and die for our redemption solely because of His great love for us. But do we really understand the depth of His love? Do we really understand? Do we even care? Do we even wish to know?

It seems that often we go out of our way to ignore God. For the most part, though, we simply forget that He is with us, watching over us, ready to lift us up when we fall, holding our hands when we are weak, embracing us when we are in need, and surrounding us with His unquenchable love. It is ironic that the more we try to push Him away, the closer He holds us in His loving arms. Like a loving parent who hugs a petulant child

---

[205] Max Lucado, *The Lucado Inspirational Reader*, 2011.

who screams *"I hate you!"* God knows that His love will overcome all bitterness and hatred, all our vitriol and blather because He knows what is truly within our hearts. He sees inside our souls. He knows that our outward screams of rage are nothing more than anger at ourselves for our own failures.

So just how much does God love us? *"But God proves his love for us in that while we were still sinners Christ died for us."*[206] While we were still sinners, He died for us. Now if that isn't love enough, it is hard to imagine what else it might be.

We might also remember, *"Who, though he was in the form of God, did not regard equality with God something to be grasped. Rather, he emptied himself, taking the form of a slave, coming in human likeness; and found human in appearance, he humbled himself, becoming obedient to death, even death on a cross."*[207] God became man, flesh and blood! From Infinite to the finite, from Immortal to the mortal, from Creator to the created, He stooped so low to give us the ultimate expression of His love.

Why did God do it? It is difficult, if not impossible, to imagine. But the next time you are present in a moment of astounding beauty such as a sunset over the mountains or a clear blue lake or the colors of a forest in autumn or the faces of family and friends, stop and listen for the voice of God. You will hear Him ask, *"Do you like it? I did it all for you out of love."*

---

[206] Rom 5:8.
[207] Phil 2:6-7.

# Those 'Aha!' moments

As the story is told, the ancient Greek scholar Archimedes, upon stepping into a bath and noticing that the water level rose suddenly, had such an epiphany that he jumped out of the bath and went running naked through the streets shouting, *"Eureka!"* What he had realized was that the volume of water displaced must be equal to the volume of the part of his body he had submerged, and that he had discovered a solution to a previously intractable problem: how to measure the volume of irregularly shaped objects with precision.

The word *'Eureka'* comes from the Ancient Greek word εὕρηκα - *heúrēka,* meaning *"I have found (it)"* which is the first person singular perfect indicative active of the verb *heuriskō* *"I find."*

Please remember what I just wrote; there will be a test later. Well, perhaps not, but what is important for us to consider is what the story of Archimedes represents, how through our lives we are often visited by serendipitous moments, those happy 'AHA!' occurrences that suddenly and unexpectedly spring into our consciousness arriving, by all appearances, from nowhere. We all have experienced such moments, and it is how we react to them and act upon them that is important. It is what we do with the revelation that makes the thought remarkable and the moment more than fleeting.

176

No matter who you are or how insignificant you might think of the idea that suddenly pops into your head, if you dismiss it and let it die without expression, it will be lost forever; it may have been of great consequence or small, but no one will benefit from it.  Consider for a moment how different the world might have been if Archimedes had simply continued with his bath and had sighed a contented "AAH!"

Our faith is often tested and revealed in serendipitous moments, and just as any other, it is how we react and the action that we take that can and will make the difference.

I recall how the words *"Go to church, you fool!"* rang so insistently through my befuddled brain at a time when I believed I had no need for God, for His Holy Church, or for any such religious foolishness. I tried so hard to resist and I could have done so, just as I had so many times before, but then I would have lost out on so much joy and happiness. No doubt my life would have been much worse for wear, and the life that dwells within my soul would be darker, devoid of His light, had I not acted upon the moment and heeded His call.

What might have been different in our lives had the two disciples, whose eyes were opened at the breaking of bread in Emmaus, stayed where they were in fear? Jesus had revealed himself to them, and they could have easily believed that they had seen a ghost, dismissed it as a hallucination and agreed to tell no one for fear of being laughed at and ridiculed. Fortunately for us, they ran back to the apostles and told them

177

*"what had taken place on the way and how he was made known to them in the breaking of bread."*[208]

A life unfulfilled is a life kept empty; a good and holy life must be filled with an unwavering faith in God and a fervent desire to fill every moment with acts of grace, mercy and love. Live your faith and act as if your life depends upon it. For it does, it really does.

# I am in God

Perhaps it is the advance of time and maturing years that moves one toward the mystical. Youth is disadvantaged by the unforeseen future that lies beyond the horizon, and thus it sees only the concrete reality of the here and now. When what lies ahead is closer than the distant ever-fading past, we find ourselves contemplating the mysterious and the unknowable, seeking answers to questions that reach out beyond our own existence. What awaits us beyond our brief moment here on earth becomes the pressing question when we come to the startling realization that the answer has somehow become an immediate, if not urgent, concern.

I find myself these days becoming more and more a student of the mystical trying to discern the "who" of God. I wish to discover His "why", His purpose for creating you and me and every one of us. I find great comfort in reading and

---

[208] Lk 24:35.

studying the mystics that have come before and have left their mark on history.

Pierre Teilhard de Chardin wrote:

*All around us, to right and left, in front and behind, above and below, we have only to go a little beyond the frontier of sensible appearances in order to see the divine welling up and showing through. But it is not only close to us, in front of us, that the divine presence has revealed itself. It has sprung up universally, and we find ourselves so surrounded and transfixed by it, that there is no room left to fall down and adore it, even within ourselves.*

*By means of all created things, without exception, the divine assails us, penetrates us and moulds us. We imagined it as distant and inaccessible, whereas in fact we live steeped in its burning layers.*[209]

What Teilhard de Chardin is telling us is that the divine is literally all around us, so much so, that we literally cannot escape being an integral part of the divine milieu of God. God is neither distant nor inaccessible primarily because *"we live steeped in its burning layers."*

*Milieu* is a French word which means one's surroundings or environment. Teilhard de Chardin says that the divine exists wherever we may look, always and everywhere, and that our

---

[209] Teilhard de Chardin, *Divine Milieu*, 2001.

milieu is in fact divine. John Kirvan adds that *"Not only was humanity where he looked, so was God. Not only is God there, but so is the fullness of our humanity. Only scratch the surface of our life and our humanity will well up and show through. So will God."*[210]

Knowing that God is close and that *"we live steeped in its burning layers"* ought to bring great comfort. We don't have to search far at all to find the divine for He is within us, He surrounds us and He fills us so *"that there is no room left to fall down and adore it, even within ourselves."*

Kwaja Abdullah Ansari wrote, *"My God, I left behind the whole world to search for you. But you were the whole world, and I could not see it."*[211] God is neither here nor there in the world. God is the world in which we live. *"We are ... no more conscious of God than we are of our own breath, it becomes a matter of ... pausing long enough to remember: 'I am breathing. I am in God. God is in me.'"*[212]

# It is God all the way to God

John Kirvan writes, *"...it is God all the way to God. God doesn't stand waiting for us till we reach the heights. God is no less present to us beginners on the first day of our journey than he is to*

---

[210] John Kirvan, *Silent Hope: Living with the Mystery of God*, 2001.
[211] Kwaja Abdullah Ansari, *Munajat*, 1089.
[212] John Kirvan, *Silent Hope: Living with the Mystery of God*, 2001.

*those whose journey has brought them to the soul's highest possibilities.*"[213]

We see God much as Michelangelo depicted Him on the ceiling of the Sistine Chapel: A stern bearded man with His finger touching the finger of Adam or with His arms outstretched dividing the waters. Of course, the image is entirely contrived since no one, least of all Michelangelo, has ever seen God, but it does serve to help us accept His existence and His power to create.

Our minds simply cannot fathom the all-encompassing presence of God, but we try anyway. We try and we try without success. It would appear as though we are incapable of quelling our insatiable desire to know God, and simply to accept fully and unconditionally His love as it is given.

A fourteenth century mystic wrote in The Cloud of Unknowing of an old monk who tells a young seeker: "*God who is our maker forever escapes our power to know. But He is forever accessible to our power to love. The power of love in each of us individually is great enough to reach him who is without limits, who forever escapes the power of our mind.*"[214]

Perhaps what we fail to grasp is bound up within the words, "*it is God all the way to God.*"

---

[213] Ibid.

[214] Carmen Acevedo Butcher, *The Cloud of Unknowing: A New Translation,* 2011.

We have all heard it said that God is always present, that He is everywhere and every when. But how much do we understand or how far are we willing to go to accept the totality of what that concept embraces?

We can conceive of God's presence as a hidden camera capturing every moment of our lives, but is that the essential essence of God's presence? God is bigger … and smaller … than that.

We have with the assistance of technology delved into the incredibly minuscule world of the atom, molecule, and smaller particles of which we are composed. No doubt our inquisitive minds will continue to discover even more infinitesimally tiny bits of ourselves.

And while we have searched for the unseen, we have also enlarged our knowledge of the universe spread across vast distances. Everywhere we look, no matter how small or how large, God is there.

We were created by God to live our lives for His glory. God has a plan for each of us and a purpose for which we are to strive with all that He has given us.

As the old monk tells the young seeker:

*There are things that God and only God can do. And we have to let go and let God do them. But if we work hard, if we press on in the task of leaving behind all that stands between us and God, then God, I promise you, will not fail you. But He is waiting for us to do our part.*

*Do not try to help him along, lest you spoil what He is attempting to do in and for you. You be the wood, He the carpenter; you the house, He its master.*[215]

# An abiding relationship with God

Pope Francis asks us, *"Do we truly pray? Without an abiding relationship with God, it is difficult to live an authentic and consistent Christian life."*[216] His words call us to consider two important thoughts, one profoundly theological and the other deeply personal.

From a theological perspective, each of us must evaluate and acknowledge the depth of our relationship with God. Toward that end, we must ask how great is our faith, how strong is our belief, and how complete is our dependency on His mercy and love. A faith without passion, without an aching desire, without an unquenchable longing for God is a faith that is dead.

Saint James tells us,

*What good is it, my brothers, if someone says he has faith but does not have works? Can that faith save him?*

---

[215] Ibid.
[216] Pope Francis (@Pontifex), October 1, 2013.

*If a brother or sister has nothing to wear and has no food for the day, and one of you says to them, 'Go in peace, keep warm, and eat well,' but you do not give them the necessities of the body, what good is it? So also faith of itself, if it does not have works, is dead.*[217]

Jesus responded to his apostles when they asked him to *"increase our faith"*[218] with a parable of the master who commanded his servant to wait on him at table with these words, *"Is he grateful to that servant because he did what was commanded? So should it be with you. When you have done all you have been commanded, say, 'We are unprofitable servants; we have done what we were obliged to do."*[219]

Simply put, it is not enough to say, *"I believe in God,"* for that requires nothing of you but rote memory and empty words. God demands more, much more. Doing only what is commanded of you will not win you any points. Just dressing out and sitting on the bench will never win you the game ball. Your relationship with God is in direct proportion to the fervency of your faith, and your fervor will only be as great as your willingness to do more than what is commanded.

To live an authentic and consistent Christian life requires you to make decisions that are incredibly personal and resolutely moral. God created each of us and gave us *"free will,"*

---

[217] Jas 2:14-17.
[218] Lk 17:5.
[219] Lk 17:9-10.

the ability to make our own choices whether they are good or bad, right or wrong.

What is often conveniently ignored or dismissed in any discussion of *"free will"* is how one must take full responsibility for one's choices. We want to be free to do anything we desire, but refuse to accept responsibility for the consequences. We therefore seek the easy way out. We try our best — or worst — to avoid making a choice. We try so hard to be agnostic and lukewarm.

What we steadfastly refuse to recognize and admit is that God abhors the wishy-washy, namby-pamby choice avoider. As Peter Kreeft states, *"The state of soul that is farthest from great sanctity is not great sin but great sluggishness. Moral lethargy is more disgusting to God than wickedness. God said that, not me. Read Revelation 3:15:16."*[220]

As Christians and children of God, we have an obligation to *"increase our faith,"* to ardently search for and attain *"an abiding relationship with God."* To know God, you must love God fervently, passionately, and completely. You must live your faith to the fullest. Your heart must be burning with a faith that is on fire with the love of God.

---

[220] Peter Kreeft, Making Choices: Practical wisdom for everyday moral decisions, 1990.

# The virtues of God

Once at a prayer service, two people rose to speak of their personal journey of faith. The first speaker was Bishop Randolph Calvo, who said that there came a moment in his youth when upon hearing church bells one day he realized that his faith and his life were one. His faith was his life and his life was his faith, and there was no separation or distinction between the two.

From this profound statement of faith, we should consider the depth and limits of our own faith. Do we live every moment of our lives with faith, in faith, and for our faith? Do we truly live what we believe? Do we live as we believe and believe as we live? As we go about our daily lives doing ordinary and at times extraordinary things, is our faith front and center, out there for everyone to see?

The second person rose to speak of her childhood and of her desire to serve God. She admitted that she struggled for years to find her way, but at every turn she always felt that something essential was missing. She had no understanding of *what* was missing. She only knew with certain confidence that God would lead her to the answer.

She spoke of the moment when she heard someone talk of having their own *"personal relationship with Jesus"* and how that word *"personal"* changed her life forever.

186

Jesus wants a *"personal relationship"* with each of us and the most important aspect of that relationship is that He wants it to be *"up close and personal."* How often do we have a conversation with Jesus? How often do you ask Him to walk with you wherever you might go? Have you ever thought to ask a neighbor to walk with you on your journey?

The message is clear. Our faith is and must be personal because our faith and our life are one. We, who have been created by God, must live our lives thanking and praising Him who has given us life.

If we separate our lives from our faith, if we hide our faith from the world, then we are denying His importance in our lives. We are trying — with utter and complete futility, I might add — to hide or disavow the Father, Son and Holy Spirit.

It is as if we are embarrassed by our faith or ashamed of Him. But what has God ever done to embarrass or shame us? All He has ever done is give us life and love us unconditionally and His *"love never fails."*[221]

As children of God, we have been given the precious gifts of faith, hope, and love. These are gifts that help us grow in our relationship with the Divine and earn a place with Him for all eternity.

---

[221] 1 Cor 13:8.

Through the gift of faith, we come to know God and believe in His Truth. As Saint Paul tells us, *"Faith is the realization of what is hoped for and evidence of things not seen."*[222] Bishop Donald Wuerl writes, *"Faith itself is a gift from God. We cannot believe in God except through the urging of the Holy Spirit. Yet we are capable of supporting and strengthening our faith life by the actions we take to build up our friendship with the LORD. It takes two to carry on a conversation, even when one of the participants is God."*[223]

The gift of hope magnifies our faith with the certain knowledge that God is always present in our lives, and that His love is eternal and unconditional.

The Catechism of the Catholic Church tells us that:

*The virtue of hope responds to the aspiration to happiness which God has placed in the heart of every man; it takes up the hopes that inspire men's activities and purifies them so as to order them to the Kingdom of heaven; it keeps man from discouragement; it sustains him during times of abandonment; it opens up his heart in expectation of eternal beatitude.*[224]

---

[222] Heb 11:1.

[223] Bishop Donald W. Wuerl, *The Catholic Way: Faith for Living Today*, September 18, 2001

[224] Catechism of the Catholic Church (CCC) #1818.

And the gift of love gives us the grace to look beyond ourselves, to love God more than we love ourselves, and to love our neighbors as much as we love ourselves.

God is love, and therefore it is through His love that we are capable of forming the most intimate of relationships.

As Saint John tells us:

*Beloved, let us love one another, because love is of God; everyone who loves is begotten by God and knows God. Whoever is without love does not know God, for God is love. In this way the love of God was revealed to us: God sent his only Son into the world so that we might have life through him. In this is love: not that we have loved God, but that he loved us and sent his Son as expiation for our sins.*

*Beloved, if God so loved us, we also must love one another. No one has ever seen God. Yet, if we love one another, God remains in us, and his love is brought to perfection in us.*[225]

The more we use these gifts, the more intimate our relationship with God will become.

---

[225] 1 Jn 4:7-12.

*"God is light, and in him there is no darkness at all."*[226] Only through Him and with Him can we pierce the darkness of sin and evil.

Built deep within our humanity is the desire to search for and to know His Truth. It is the nature of man to crave the light and to desire an intimate personal relationship with our Creator.

The Gospel of John describes our relationship with God at its outset:

> *In the beginning was the Word, and the Word was with God, and the Word was God. All things came to be through Him, and without him nothing came to be. What came to be through him was life, and this life was the light of the human race; the light shines in the darkness, and the darkness has not overcome it.*[227]

Jesus tells us, *"I am the light of the world. Whoever follows me will not walk in darkness, but will have the light of life"*[228] and at yet at another time he tells his disciples, *"While I am in the world, I am the light of the world."*[229] Through the light of Christ, we can see all that is good and can grow in our relationship to God.

---

[226] 1 Jn 1:5.
[227] Jn 1:1-5.
[228] Jn 8:12.
[229] Jn 9:5.

The second speaker left us with a brief poem attributed to Saint Francis of Assisi that offers much for us to ponder and to pray:

*Such love does the sky now pour,*
*that whenever I stand in a field,*
*I have to wring out the light*
*when I get home.*

God is with us and always present for us, but all too often we push Him away. We are blinded by the darkness, unable to see the brilliance of His glory. We are deafened by the siren sounds of evil, unable and unwilling to hear the purest melody of His voice.

# Miracle and majesty

We live in a world at a time where miracle and majesty have become fantasy and mundane. Our senses have been numbed by the constant barrage of the unbelievable and the bizarre to the point where we no longer see or believe in miracles. Our sight has become so diminished by optic overload from digitally-enhanced movies and video games that we have become blind to the awesome beauty and majesty of God's creation. Our minds have been corrupted and filled with dark and forbidding images from books, films, and games that focus on the evil rather than the good.

Our increasingly secular culture promotes a materialistic attitude that denigrates and dismisses the idea of miracles and

191

mysteries. Like the apostle Thomas, unless we can see it, touch it, taste it, or can prove it, then it cannot possibly exist or be real. Mysteries and miracles are suspect, only real when scientifically or rationally explained. This materialistic attitude directs us toward the denial of the unknowable, to admitting that creation, redemption, resurrection, sin, grace, and the presence of God are improbabilities, if not impossibilities, not reality.

The sense of wonder that should fill us has been replaced by relativistic pragmatism and materialism. We see the light but hold onto the darkness, afraid to believe what we cannot prove and hungry for that which we cannot grasp within our physical senses. Without mystery or miracle, without the unknowable, we submit ourselves to the darkness that surrounds us and close our eyes to the beauty of the light that is God.

We have lost our moral compass. We have lost our capacity to feel and to understand the difference between right and wrong, moral and immoral, good versus evil. Heroes have been replaced by villains, evil wins over good, honor and decency are weaknesses, lies have replaced the truth, reality is no longer relevant, and faith and God are for the ignorant and uninformed. Today is an Orwellian 1984 more than thirty years after the fact.

A few years ago, a small group of teenage boys was attending a three-day confirmation retreat. The group was comprised mostly of inner-city youth who had never been far away from their neighborhoods; none had ever been to the pristine blue waters of the beautiful lake nestled high in the majestic mountains.

Shortly after lunch on Saturday, they were led by a young priest to the shores of the lake strewn with immense boulders worn smooth by the waters and the passage of time. Arriving at a point that provided a panoramic view of the lake and the mountains that surrounded it, the priest asked the boys to find a seat on the rocks. He had prepared a few remarks but then, just before he began to speak, he paused. Gazing at all the beauty that surrounded them, he told the group that rather than him talking, he had decided to give up his time to God. He asked the boys ranging in age between thirteen and fifteen, full of youthful energy and restlessness, to spend thirty minutes in silence, quietly listening to what God might have to say to each one of them.

There are miracles, big and small, that happen every day. All we have to do is open our eyes to see them and our hearts to experience them. That day was filled, filled with miracles, some ancient and some new.

For thirty minutes there was total silence. There was no noise other than the soft lapping of the waves against the shore and the gentle whisper of a breeze caressing the trees. There was no movement except for the slow studied swivel of heads and youthful eyes absorbing the ancient majesty and the wondrous miracle of all that God had created. Young, rambunctious, energetic teenagers were miraculously enthralled and transfixed with awesome wonder and pure amazement at what He had created. God spoke and they listened. And each heard His voice.

There was another miracle present that day, although few recognized it or even knew of it. The priest that led that group of boys over those huge boulders had only one leg, having lost a leg in a gang fight when he was a teenager. Raised in the inner city, he had gravitated to the gang life at an early age.

He had lost his leg and nearly his life, but then God found him and he found God. He came to realize that God had given him a second chance and an opportunity to replace what he had lost with something good. He became a priest helping others like him to find God.

That day at the lake in the mountains, God found him and those boys found God. And those were miracles.

# Chapter Nine

## One of the least of these

*And the king will say in reply,*
*'Amen, I say to you, whatever you did*
*for one of these least brothers of mine,*
*you did for me'.*

Matt 26:40

When we look outside ourselves and see, really see, the presence of God in all and everything, then we will begin the wonderful voyage of discovery and budding awareness of the Voices of God. The Voices of God are constantly speaking to us in a cacophony of joyful noise. God is never silent, He has never been silent, and He will never be silent.

Look around. Really look around you and you will not only hear God, you will see God. God is present everywhere, all the time. He is in you and He is in me. He is in the best of us; He is in the worst of us. He is in the greatest of us; He is in the least of us.

# Parousia Personified

The word 'Parousia' is a transliteration of the Greek παρουσία and in classical Greek it means or implies a *presence* or an *arrival*. Saint Paul often used it to indicate his own presence or impending arrival somewhere such as Corinth or Philippi. In the early church, Christians believed that the end time, coupled with God's final judgment, was imminent and that they would know it by the second coming of the Son of Man, Jesus Christ. Early Christians called this event "*the Parousia*" or "*the day of the Lord.*"

More than two-thousand years have passed, and Christians throughout the world continue to believe in and await the Parousia event, although with perhaps a slightly longer outlook as to when. But no one knows when God will have had enough and no one can predict when Parousia will occur.

Very few today will profess or proclaim that the end time is near although many will admit that these times are assuredly not heavenly. And most would agree that our times are in desperate need of salvation, but then that has been essentially true since God created man and all things.

Choose any period of time throughout human history and you will find a plethora of examples of man's inhumanity, at times more predominant than at other times, but never completely absent. Even God's only attempt to purge humanity of its self-annihilating inhumanity by destroying all of mankind, with the exception of Noah and his family, failed to eradicate our concupiscence.

What we can also surmise and assume is that the preponderance of the human race will not be physically present when Parousia finally arrives; most of us, along with all of our ancestors, will have long left this mortal life for a spiritual and eternal one. But whether mortal or immortal, all will await Parousia and the final judgment of God. How we will be judged will be predicated entirely on how we have lived our lives while on this earth.

At the final judgment, *"when the Son of Man comes in his glory,"*[230] Jesus tells us that we will be separated by how we have

---

[230] Mt 26:31.

treated others. That should be worth at least a moment's consideration. We will be judged not by how much wealth we have accumulated, nor by the fame we have acquired, nor by the power we have attained, nor by how well we have behaved, but rather we will be judged *solely* by how we have treated our fellow man: family, friends, enemies, neighbors, and strangers.

Jesus said, *"Amen, I say to you, whatever you did for one of these least brothers of mine, you did for me."*[231] And perhaps in anticipation of our modern day tendency toward nuanced pettifoggery, Jesus restates this in the negative so as to leave us absolutely no wiggle room by saying, *"Amen, I say to you, what you did not do for one of these least ones, you did not do for me."*[232]

Seeking reward in this life is self-defeating, just as the rich man discovered when he died, for he had been rewarded and would now be forever tormented.[233] We should constantly remind ourselves that whatever we do or do not do for others will be for our own benefit and our own salvation. Yet ultimately it is all for God.

## Knowledge is brain food

Eliezer ben Hurcanus was a first and second century rabbi who was known to tell his disciples to *"Repent one day before your death."* And when asked, *"How will we know when that*

---

[231] Mt 26:40.
[232] Mt 26:45.
[233] Lk 16:19-31.

*day is?"* he would reply, *"All the more reason to repent today, lest you die tomorrow."*[234]

We are all called to seek the wisdom of God and to see the world as He sees it. God should be the source of all our wisdom. But today people seek a different kind of wisdom, a secular and self-centered knowledge rather than the truth that comes from God.

Knowledge is brain food but wisdom is soul food.  The gift of wisdom in Latin is *'sapida scientia'* which means *"tasted knowledge."* Wisdom cannot be obtained from a book or learned in a classroom. Rather it comes from within, from the soul. Wisdom is not knowing what one values but rather valuing that which is worth knowing.

But just what is Wisdom? Is it sound judgment or a sharp intellect? I personally believe it is the act of making wise choices, choosing between what is good and right rather than what is opportunistic and self-indulgent. Wisdom presumes that we are prepared for the unexpected, able to anticipate and put ourselves in the best position to act wisely when the unexpected happens, and ready to wait with sure confidence that we have done all that we could and should have done.

---

[234] Eliezer ben Hurcanus is the sixth most frequently mentioned sage in the Mishnah, a severe conservative whose teachings were often at odds with his contemporaries and was excommunicated for heresy. Though excommunicated, Rabbi Eliezer is quoted in the Mishnah, the Baraita, and the Talmud more frequently than any one of his contemporaries. He was also the author of *The Ethics of Rabbi Eliezer*.

Wisdom comes when we overcome our desire for power, possessions, and pleasure and learn to live as Christ commands us to live, by loving one another and worshipping God every minute of every day. The more we seek a perfect relationship with God, the more His wisdom will hasten to us, and the more wisdom will graciously appear in our souls.

All too often we fail to prepare ourselves for the unexpected. We live in the moment without any thought for tomorrow. We believe we have all the time in the world to reach a goal, break or make a habit, build a relationship, eat right, exercise more, or to do all those things that we would love to do but haven't had the opportunity to accomplish. Many of us have even developed "bucket lists" – things to do before we die. But exactly how many of us have actually acted upon them?

Jesus tells us always to be prepared and to *"stay awake, for you know neither the day nor the hour."*[235] Only God knows and He isn't talking. Despite wishful thinking, the fact is that we neither can nor will know the time or place for ourselves or for anyone else.

One of my favorite ministries is to visit the elderly and the homebound and to offer them the opportunity to receive our LORD in Holy Communion. Most of those I visit range in age from eighty to ninety-eight years young. Believe me no one there has a clue when God will call them home.

---

[235] Mt 25:13.

My parents died in an accident when they were fifty-eight and fifty-nine years old. They were healthy and expected to live many more years. After all, they still had children at home.

My youngest daughter once asked me to offer prayers for someone she knew. She wrote, *"Andrew is someone I work with who was recently released from the hospital on hospice care with colon cancer. He is 38 years old and has two boys, Ben and Cooper, ages 9 and 7. Dad, I know you've said life's not fair, but it's really not fair that a 38-year old has to say goodbye to his wife and two boys."*

My father's oldest brother, and my namesake, was killed at the age of twelve in a hunting accident.

We all know someone who has died. Rarely has death arrived when expected and few had the opportunity to say goodbye or adequately to prepare for it.

We all have things we regret or wish we could do over. We have many opportunities to do the right thing and to correct the mistakes we have made, but too often we miss the moment and simply let things slide. After all, we say, there is always tomorrow.

No one on their death bed wishes they had spent more time at work or regrets not having kept a cleaner house. What we do regret is far more important and far less tangible. We regret not saying, *"I'm sorry."* We regret not saying, *"I love you."* We regret not stopping to *"smell the roses,"* not spending time with those we love, helping those who are in need, giving the gift of time to others, or spending time with God. Like the foolish young women in the Gospel,[236] we burn our oil on things that do not matter and fail to pack extra flasks of oil for contingencies.

We need to be watchful while we wait, to pay attention, and prepare to act at the appointed time: when a stranger needs a hand, when someone needs your time, when God gives you a call. The key is to be prepared — and that is wisdom. While we can determine neither the day nor the hour, we must be ready for it every moment of our lives. To be wise, then, is not to try to calculate the appointed day or time, but to spend the present moment — now — as if it were your last and to ask the question *"Am I ready to meet God?"* Or perhaps more importantly *"Am I ready for God to meet me?"*

# An openness to love

*"Children,"* Saint John writes, *"let us love not in word or speech but in deed and truth."*[237] We generally think of love as an emotion or a feeling, or of being in love. But while there are feelings associated with love, love is not a feeling. Jesus tells us to love one another, not through our feelings but by our actions and how we live our lives.

---

[236] Mt 25:1-13.
[237] 1 Jn 3:18.

In his book Love and Responsibility, Pope Saint John Paul II writes that love consists of three actions: Seeing the good in others, doing good for others, and allowing others to love you.[238]

We cannot love another without seeing the good in them. And although it is difficult at times to find the good in others, we must remember first and foremost that God created us all. We are His children so it is always possible to find some good. After all, God does. We just have to see them as God sees them.

In order for us to love others, we must do good for them. Once, as the owner of a small software company, I wore a T-shirt that had printed on the front *"I am the boss,"* and on the back, *"so how can I help you today?"*

In order to do good for others we must become the servant and not the master in the same way that Jesus did when he washed his disciples' feet. We must ask the questions: *"How can I help you? What can I do for you?"* That is the true essence of love. It implies that we are placing ourselves completely at and in the service of others and especially to the service of God.

As Saint Paul tells us:

*I urge you therefore, brothers, by the mercies of God, to offer your bodies as a living sacrifice, holy and pleasing to God, your spiritual worship. Do not conform*

---

[238] Karol Wojtyla (Pope Saint John Paul II), *Love and Responsibility*, Ignatius Press, 1993.

*yourself to this age but be transformed by the renewal of your mind, that you may discern what is the will of God, what is good and pleasing and perfect.*[239]

Love also demands an openness to being loved. This requires making ourselves vulnerable and that can often be especially difficult. We may think being vulnerable means to show weakness or to open ourselves to attack. But we must be willing to embrace the possibility of pain and suffering if we are to open ourselves to being loved.

Loving, not merely in words but in truth and in deed, is not easy. We can never do this on our own. The energy to love comes to us from the One who loves us unconditionally.

Saint Paul tells us many times that Christ is the head and we are the body:

*For as in one body we have many parts, and all the parts do not have the same function, so we, though many, are one body in Christ and individually parts of one another.*"[240] "*As a body is one though it has many parts, and all the parts of the body, though many, are one body, so also Christ.*[241]

Our unity and our oneness with Jesus Christ are often difficult to describe.

---

[239] Rm 12:1-2.
[240] Rm 12:4-5.
[241] 1 Cor 12:12.

Meister Eckhart said,

*If anyone put water in a barrel, the barrel would surround the water, but the water would not be in the barrel [i.e. it would not occupy the same space as the wood of the barrel], nor would the barrel be in the water: but the soul is wholly one with God...In spiritual things there is no separating of one from another.*[242]

This is what the parable of the vine and the branches means. Just as the life of the branch is derived from the vine, so too the love that we have within us comes from remaining connected to God. Without God we are like broken branches drying out in the sun, brittle and useless. But if we begin by loving God and seeing how good He is and then giving our body and soul completely over to serve Him in worship, and if we then allow Him to love us in return, we can never be detached from the vine because the infinite life-giving energy that comes from God will fill us and overflow into our love of others.

# Shema Israel!

A scholar of the Law asks Jesus of the 613 laws written in the Torah which is the most important.[243] Now this is a trick

---

[242] Meister Eckhard, The Kingdom of Heaven with You – Volume I, translated by C. M. Vega.
[243] Mt 22:36.

question, for no matter which one Jesus picks, he will be judged as answering incorrectly since, to the Pharisees, all the laws were considered to be of equal importance. This is like a mother who picks two shirts for her son — a blue one and a red one — and asks which one he likes the best. He says he likes both of them equally. She asks him to put one of them on. So he puts on the blue one and his mother says, *"So you don't like the red one?"*

Instead of choosing one law as most important, Jesus responds with two and neither two are from among the expected 613 laws.

The first and most important commandment that Jesus quotes is from Deuteronomy. It is called the 'Shema Israel' which is, *"Hear, O Israel: The LORD is our God, the LORD alone! Therefore, you shall love the LORD, your God, with all your heart, and with all your soul, and with all your strength."*[244] Fervent Jews pray this at least twice a day. By reciting it during their daily chores, they become more aware of God's presence while remembering that the most important thing in their life is to love God above everything and everyone.

The second one is from Leviticus, *"You shall love your neighbor as yourself."*[245] Matthew is not the only place where we find that Jesus combined the commandments to love God and neighbor. All three of the Synoptic Gospels recount Jesus doing

---

[244] Dt 6:4-5.
[245] Lv 19:17.

so,[246] indicating how strongly Jesus believed this to be true. Saint John emphasizes its importance when he writes, *"If anyone says, 'I love God,' but hates his brother, he is a liar; for whoever does not love a brother whom he has seen cannot love God whom he has not seen. This is the commandment we have from him: whoever loves God must also love his brother."*[247]

Jesus taught us that we must love even our enemies. *"You have heard that it was said, 'You shall love your neighbor and hate your enemy.' But I say to you, love your enemies and pray for those who persecute you, that you may be children of your heavenly Father, for He makes his sun rise on the bad and the good, and causes rain to fall on the just and the unjust."*[248]

God is love and everything He does flows from his love for us. God's love tempers everything He does, including His justice, mercy, kindness, and goodness. The love of God comes first and the love of neighbor is firmly grounded in the love of God. The more we know of God's love and truth, the more we love what He loves and reject what is hateful and contrary to his will.

As God's love makes a home in us, we reach out to love the people that God brings into our lives. As Saint John tells us, it is a contradiction to say I love God and turn away from a

---

[246] Mt 22:37-40, Mk 12:29-31. Lk 10:27.
[247] 1 Jn 4:20.21.
[248] Mt 5:43-45.

brother, a sister, or a neighbor.[249] Love is not a prize to be hoarded but a gift to be given away. If we love God who first loved us, it always leads us to love those around us.

To love God with one's whole heart means to give our wholehearted *yes* to life and all that life brings with it. It means to accept without reservation all which God has ordained for one's life. It means to have the attitude that Jesus had when he said, *"Father, if you are willing, take this cup away from me; still, not my will but yours be done."*[250] To love God with one's whole heart is to make one's own the words of Dag Hammarsjold who said, *"For all that has been, Thanks. To all that we shall be, Yes."*[251]

# An Unclean Spirit

While Jesus was teaching in the synagogue, a man with an unclean spirit challenged him, heckled him, and disrupted his teaching moment. Most of us can likewise recall instances where a meeting or presentation was disrupted by someone who disagreed with what was being said or who had their own agenda to promote. Few of us can forget the horrific results of the terrorist attacks on 9-11, the Oklahoma bombings, Columbine, or the shooting of Congresswoman Gabrielle Giffords.

---

[249] 1 Jn 4:20.

[250] Lk 22:42.

[251] Dag Hammarsjold, Swedish Diplomat, United Nations Secretary-General, and Nobel Peace Prize recipient, *Markings, Journal Entries*, 1964.

Evil exists in this world, and no matter how much we wish it did not, it remains. Albert Einstein once said that *"The real problem is in the hearts and minds of men. It is easier to denature plutonium than to denature the evil spirit of man."*[252] We are, as human beings, sinners both by inclination and in fact. We are all born with the stain of original sin on our soul, a legacy inherited from our first parents. Fortunately, baptism cleanses our souls. Unfortunately, the inclination to sin still remains.

We tend to overdramatize this incident in the Gospel and to imagine a scene like that in The Exorcist with spinning heads and shrieking utterances in strange tongues. Our imaginations run wild, and we conjure up demonic possession or we suspect some form of physical disability like epilepsy or perhaps a mental issue like schizophrenia.

I suspect the reality is far more mundane and, unfortunately, all too common. In a very real sense, each of us has within us unclean spirits, spirits that, for the most part, are kept under control and hidden from others. We each have a soul within us, an immortal spirit. It is what defines us as human beings, creatures made in the image and likeness of God. When we sin – and we all sin – we defile our souls and in doing so we become like the man in the Gospel, a person with an unclean spirit.

---

[252] Albert Einstein, *The Real Problem Is In the Hearts of Men*, The New York Times, Sunday Magazine, June 23, 1946.

What caused the man to confront Jesus? Why did he cry out, *"What have you to do with us, Jesus of Nazareth?"*[253] Somewhere deep inside he must have realized that Jesus could save him, could rid him of his unclean spirits, could make him whole and clean again. Jesus knew his heart, saw within his soul, and cleaned away the darkness that he kept hidden away. Jesus saw the unclean spirit of the man and commanded, *"Quiet! Come out of him!"*[254]

We all have secrets, thoughts and experiences that we don't wish to share with anyone, things that we fervently hope will never be revealed. We all have our indiscretions, faults, and failures and we file them away. We place them in boxes in the forgotten recesses of our minds, all the while believing that once forgotten they will never be found again.

The problem is that what we so desperately wish to keep hidden and safe from all around us cannot be kept from God. He knows. He has always known and He even knows where you stored them.

And then there is another problem. We know. We cannot simply forget what we have done or failed to do. Over time, all our secrets, sins, and failings overshadow the good that is within. Like monsters hiding under the bed or in the closet that terrify in the darkness we begin to believe that we are so flawed and broken that nothing can ever save us. We stumble through

---

253 Mk 1:24.
254 Mk 1:25.

life believing that we are unforgivable and unworthy. We see ourselves as total failures. We become so ashamed of whom we are and what we have done, that we find ourselves, like Adam and Eve, hiding from God in our newly discovered nakedness.

No matter how hard we attempt to hide our unclean spirits, they bring clutter to our soul, dampen our spirit, and build walls that restrict our personal relationship with God.

Instead of holding onto those secrets that dirty and tarnish our souls, Jesus asks us to give our sins over to him and to let him clean our souls and make us whole again. But that requires us to recognize that He is in control and that we are vulnerable. And that is often very difficult to accept and even more difficult to do, for most of us like being in control. We feel uncomfortable when we are not behind the wheel, when we are dependent on another. The thought of handing control over to someone else can be frightening to say the least.

To be vulnerable to Christ is like a new-born infant being held in the loving arms of his or her mother. The child is entirely dependent on another, completely vulnerable and unable to exert any control or to make any decisions. And yet the infant intuitively understands that he or she is safe and loved.

Like an infant, we should intuitively know that we are safe in God's hands. God loves us and wants us to love Him in return. No matter how many times we fall, He will always forgive us as long as we ask for His forgiveness. With Jesus in control, unclean spirits don't stand a chance and good always wins out over evil.

# He is waiting for the butterfly

Within every caterpillar lies a butterfly, a creature whose beauty far surpasses the life that dies so that it may endow the earth with a singular moment of wonder and awe.

Bertrand Russell wrote that an honest philosophy could not reasonably deny that *"no fire, no heroism, no intensity of thought and feeling can preserve an individual life beyond the grave. All the labors of the ages, all the devotion, all the inspiration, all the noonday brightness of human genius are destined to extinction in the vast death of the solar system."*[255] Obviously, he failed to see the butterfly within and the soul which is the image of God. His view was like a man who has the gift of sight but chooses to be blinded so he can avoid the inevitable truth that comes with the light of day.

How sad it is to read or hear of those who have no expectation beyond the grave or belief in God or hope in perpetual joy with Him. For those who do not believe, they live only in the larval stage, doomed to crawl on this earth for a brief time without any promise of bursting forth into a beauty that soars beyond the bounds of earth. How sad, how hopelessly sad.

---

[255] Bertrand Russell, *A Free Man's Worship*, 1903.

Perhaps to be a lowly caterpillar is not so bad when imagining the life that has been promised and the life that is yet to come. Our lives are filled with many temptations, and in our susceptibility and concupiscence we often expend far too much energy and effort overindulging in the bounty that surrounds us. We forget our temporality and earthly purpose and, through weakness, shove aside thoughts of our Creator. We sin and sin and then sin some more.

If you were asked this question: *"What is the longest you have gone without sinning? A week, a day, an hour?"* how would you respond? Most of us, if we would be completely honest with ourselves, would say, *"I can't live a day without sinning."* We would be ignoring the truth and fooling ourselves if we were to say that we had not sinned in thought or action for the day or the week. Saint John says:

> *If we say, "We are without sin," we deceive ourselves, and the truth is not in us. If we acknowledge our sins, He is faithful and just and will forgive our sins and cleanse us from every wrongdoing. If we say, "We have not sinned," we make him a liar, and his word is not in us*[256]

God created us and He wants us to be the best that we can be. He knows that we are imperfect creatures and that we will often, even daily, falter and sin. But He created us and He loves us despite our faults, lapses, and failures. Why? Because

---

[256] 1 Jn 1:8-10.

He knows that we are more than this physical shell which will one day return to dust. He knows that we are destined to be more and become more. He knows that we will ultimately die to this mortal life so as to live with Him for all eternity, singing His praises forever.

God, in His own perfection, knows that we are imperfect creatures, but then He created us that way. He will always forgive us. All we have to do is ask Him, no matter how often that might be. After all, He is waiting for the butterfly to fly home.

# God loves the sinner

One of the most memorable and often quoted lines from the movie **Forrest Gump** is, *"My momma always said 'Life is like a box of chocolates ... you never know what you're going to get.'"*[257] There is truth within this metaphor that goes beyond the fact that we cannot foresee what lies ahead in life. There is much more that lies beyond our poor abilities to sense, to feel, to see, and to understand. What lies within the soul is forever hidden from human eyes, but God sees. God knows and He loves you anyway.

We are all sinners. No one is without sin except God. Sin tarnishes and damages the soul. Jesus became man and he suffered and died so that our sins would be forgiven. His life

---

[257] From the 1994 movie Forrest Gump.

was and is a testament to God's unwavering desire to forgive sin and to unconditionally love the sinner. While only partially scriptural, the saying "*God loves the sinner but hates the sin*" accurately describes God's love for us. Peter Kreeft, says:

> *This is not a hairsplitting, abstract, technical distinction for scholars and theologians. It is crucial and practical. If we love the sin, we do **not** love the sinner, just as if we love the cancer, we do not love the patient.*
>
> *There is a proper kind of hate. Even God has 'wrath' (unless Scripture lies). God does not hate any **sinner**, not even the worst. Jesus loved Judas to the last, and called him 'friend.' God loves Stalin and Hitler and Charles Manson, as David loved his rebel son Absalom, and for the same reason: He is our Father. But God hates sin, and so should we. To hate **people** is to lack compassion.*[258]

If we doubt God's love for the sinner and His hatred for sin, all we have to do is recall all the sinners (remember we are all sinners) who have become saints despite their sinfulness. Saint Paul, the apostle to the Gentiles, imprisoned and condemned those who followed Jesus. Yet God loved him and forgave him. Saint Augustine, a Doctor of the Church, was guilty of living a hedonistic lifestyle and, for a period of time,

---

[258] Peter Kreeft, *Making Choices: Practical wisdom for everyday moral decisions*, 1990.

was a pagan and a follower of several heretical cults. Yet God loved him and forgave him. Saint Francis of Assisi was a wealthy young man who was known for his love of the many pleasures in life and was a soldier for a time. Yet God loved him and forgave him. Saint Ignatius of Loyola was a proud and vain young man who sought glory in battle and the killing of those who were not Christian. Yet God loved him and forgave him.

All saints are and were sinners simply because we, all of humanity, are sinners. What set them apart and what made them saints was that they came to love the sinner but hate the sin. They discovered the truth that comes to light only through the humble recognition of their own fragile humanity, and that all they had been given was a gift freely given by their Creator. They recognized and admitted that all they had achieved and whatever they had gained had come from God and not through their sole power. They learned that *"whoever exalts himself will be humbled, and the one who humbles himself will be exalted."*[259]

# Produce good fruit

In his novel Love Story, Erich Segal has Jennifer Cavilleri tell Oliver Barrett, *"Love means never having to say you're sorry."*[260] While this sounds like a perfectly lovely sentiment, sure to bring a tear to the eye and a sigh to the lips, it falls far short of what is honest and true. We all fail, for we are imperfect creatures who,

---

[259] Lk 18:14.
[260] Erich Segal, *Love Story*, 1970,

216

through our imperfections, frequently fall short. No matter how great our love might be, we must always say *'I'm sorry'* when we fail.

Acknowledgement and acceptance of our faults and failures is both necessary and important, but it is never enough. Apologies are never enough. Asking for forgiveness is never enough. Saying 'I'm sorry' is never enough.

When we ask God for His forgiveness for our sins, we are required to go beyond simply saying "I'm sorry," we must be truly repentant, honestly promise to sin no more, avoid the near occasion of sin, and make restitution or penance for the wrongs that we have committed. In other words, we must do more. We must make appropriate changes in our behavior. We must change our lives.

Like Jesus, John the Baptist knew the hearts and minds of the Pharisees and Sadducees and like Jesus, called them to task for their pride and arrogance. He told them, *"Produce good fruit as evidence of your repentance."*[261] Saint Matthew used the Greek μετάνόος (*metánoeō*) in the nuanced meaning to *"think life over again,"* that is, to make the appropriate and necessary changes to one's life. John was therefore telling those who came to be baptized that they must, in addition to acknowledging their sins, change their lives in significant and positive ways. Words without actions will never be enough.

---

[261] Mt 3:8.

No matter where we are in our lives, there is always room for improvement.

A dear friend asked how he could know that he was doing all that he was supposed to do to live as God wanted him to live. I told him that everyone feels inadequate when standing before God, and that no one can ever say *"I am worthy."* No matter who we are or how we live our lives, we can and must always do more, for that is what God requires of us. It is never easy, but then it was never intended to be so. Sinner or saint, we always have to do more, to try harder to *"be perfect, just as your heavenly Father is perfect."*[262]

The first step is to stop sinning – to fervently and deliberately – turn away from a sinful life. As it is for an addict, the first step is acknowledgement and acceptance. The next step is to live in the good, to change the very act of living, and to seek out the positive and the holy. And finally, when your life exemplifies the holy, you must rise up to the challenge that lies in becoming a saint.

## We are spiritual beings

Pierre Teilhard de Chardin wrote, *"We are not human beings having a spiritual experience. We are spiritual beings having a human experience."*[263]

---

[262] Mt 5:48.
[263] Pierre Teilhard de Chardin, *Divine Milieu*, 2001.

What Teilhard de Chardin offers is a refreshing perspective on our existence that few have ever considered. Common wisdom speaks through our human experience, through our hearts and minds. We acknowledge the existence of our soul even though we cannot touch, hold, feel, or see that which defines who we are. We do not comprehend that, created in the image and likeness of God, our true nature belongs among the eternal and the spiritual.

We see ourselves as the egg without any understanding or comprehension of the life that exists beyond the shell and of the life that coexists within something so much greater. We differentiate ourselves from the rest of God's creation by pronouncing that we are greater because we have a soul. We argue that we are human because within us exists a spirit that elevates us beyond the ordinary.

It is our human conceit that allows us to believe that the spirit lies within our humanity and that our soul's existence is dependent upon our coming into being. What arrogance! Our souls will live forever outside of time with or without our bodies and our humanity. While it is true that our bodies will one day be reunited with our souls, it is that interregnum, that period of separation of our mortal bodies and our immortal souls that elevates the soul. It is our soul, our spiritual being that envelops and embodies our human experiences.

It is our soul that is closest to God. It is our spirit that experiences far more than we can or ever will experience as human beings. Our human experiences are but a small portion of the wonder of our creation, and it is in our understanding of this that we can begin to prioritize and order our lives here on this earth.

A sign outside a small rural church states, *"Make God your first priority, not your last resort."* It is important that we see ourselves, both human and spirit, in the proper perspective. We must let our spirit, which is our soul, lead the way to holiness and to God.

Teilhard de Chardin believed that all we do in life, whether religious or secular, when performed at our best leads to holiness. He dismissed the notion held by many over the past two centuries that only the religious could be *"holy"*. He believed that all work, both religious and secular, is an essential component of creation and the Incarnation and therefore should be offered up for the glory of God.

It is the spirit that drives us toward holiness and toward God. It is the spirit that contains our humanity and it is the spirit that holds all that we are and all that we will ever be. The human mind and heart are far too limited to go much beyond the search for sustenance and ordinary living. When we free ourselves from the idea that the soul lies within our greater selves and allow our spirit to lead us and to take in all that we experience, then we will have come to terms with all of who and what we truly are. And when we do come to such a moment, we will understand that we are spiritual beings having human experiences.

# Find the time

Gisele Bundchen once said, *"Everyone has an hour in their day to go and do something for somebody else; I don't care how busy they are."*[264] While I'm sure that there will be those who would disagree with her, it is certainly an idea worth serious consideration.

Most of us in the normal course of any given day do something for ourselves or our families that could easily and simply be expanded to help others with little additional effort on our part. Case in point: after a recent snowstorm, as a man was clearing his driveway with a snow blower, he noticed a neighbor clearing her driveway with a snow shovel. It took less than five minutes for him to clear hers. He went on to clear another neighbor's driveway who he knew had spent the night clearing nearby highways. It took but a few minutes of his time to complete the task. Fifteen minutes of his time. Time he didn't miss.

There are many ways that we can help others, no matter how busy we believe we are. The most important thing to consider is how what we are about to do might benefit others. It really is that simple and, in most cases, it costs no more than a

---

[264] Gisele Bundchen, wife of Tom Brady, quarterback for the New England Patriots.

few minutes of our time. But to the recipient it will be a wonderful and priceless gift.

Over the past few years, I have had the great honor to know and work with a wonderful group of people who regularly give of their time to others. Not once have I heard a complaint or demurral; rather what is always expressed is joy and immense satisfaction. Who are these givers of time who unselfishly give of themselves to help others? They are your neighbors and fellow parishioners who serve at Church as Sacristans, Lectors, and Extraordinary Ministers of Holy Communion. They are those who lend their voices in song while serving in the choir. They are those who take the time to visit and take Holy Communion to the elderly and homebound. They are those who offer their time to help our students at our school. They are those who give an hour or two to stuff envelopes, count money, or clean and decorate the church. They are those who gift us with their marvelous cooking skills by providing us with many delicious meals.

With few exceptions, these willing volunteers and donators of time and treasure provide immeasurable benefit to others without expending a great deal of time on their part. We owe each of them an enormous debt of gratitude, although few if any wish to be acknowledged for their service because they don't do it for any recognition or even an expression of gratitude. They do it because they see a need. They do it for love of their neighbor. They do it for the joy they see in the eyes and faces of those they serve.

If asked why they do it they will give you different responses but perhaps they are reminded that

> ...God so loved the world that He gave his only Son, so that everyone who believes in him might not perish but might have eternal life.[265]

No one should feel compelled to make such a sacrifice, but an hour of your time should be more than doable.

## Go with God's Blessing

The 13th-century mystic, Blessed Angela of Foligno, had a deep experience of God. When her confessor asked her to tell him about it, she said, *"Father, if you experienced what I experienced and then you had to stand in the pulpit to preach, you could only say to the people, 'My friends, go with God's blessing, because today I can say nothing to you about God.'"*[266]

In Exodus, God revealed His proper personal name to Moses, *"I am who am. ...This is what you shall tell the Israelites: I AM sent me to you. ...This is my name forever, this is my title for all generations."*[267] In Hebrew, God's name is formed by an unpronounceable string of consonants (YHWH or יהוה) and this name is considered so holy that it must never be pronounced.

---

[265] Jn 3:16.
[266] Blessed Angela of Foligno, *Book of Visions and Instructions*.
[267] Ex 3:14-15.

It is altogether a wonderful thing to have a name for God that must never be pronounced. We Christians don't talk or think like that but we say something that is even more radical. For us it is not that there is some single word that must never be uttered but that all words fall short. Use any words you like or as many as you like but know that when you have uttered them, all you have said is absolutely nothing at all. This is something that is not stated clearly or often enough.

Saint Thomas Aquinas wrote that "*Whatever is comprehended by a finite being [that is, us] is itself finite.*"[268]

God is a dark mystery. But isn't God light? "*God is light and in him there is no darkness at all.*"[269] Yes, but as Saint Augustine explains, excess of light has the same effect as darkness.

Henri Nouwen tells us in his spiritual masterpiece The Return of the Prodigal Son,[270] that as persons who understand ourselves as already committed we still need to make a three-fold conversion movement:

1) We need to move from being a bystander to being a participant;
2) from being a judge to being a repentant sinner; and
3) from speaking about love to actually letting ourselves be loved.

---

[268] St. Thomas Aquinas, *Summa Theologica.*
[269] 1 Jn 1:5.
[270] Henri J. M. Nouwen, *The Return of the Prodigal Son,* 1994.

What is involved in each of these?

From being a bystander to being a participant: In essence, what we must do is to move from studying life, speaking about it, teaching about it, writing about it, and perhaps even at times mimicking it, to actually living it. I know this sounds very much like a cliché devoid of substance, but a lot of what is wrong in the world, in the church, and within our personal lives is precisely the fact that we study things, talk about them, and strongly voice our convictions about them but often do little or nothing about them.

For example, we do not lack for literature, moral rhetoric, or good analysis on social justice, but there is very little being done. This is not so much because our passion for justice is insincere, but because at the end of the day, we are too frequently bystanders and not participants.

The same holds true for prayer. There is no shortage of literature in this area (and no shortage of workshops either). We talk enough about prayer. We just don't pray a lot. In terms of deep private prayer, we pray very little. Again we are much more in the position of the bystander than participant. Saint Therese of Lisieux once wrote: "*I always preferred to pray rather than to have spiritual conversations about prayer.*"[271]

We must also move from being judge to being a repentant sinner. What is meant by this? Many, if not most, of

---

[271] Saint Therese of Lisieux, Doctor of the Church, *The Story of a Soul*, 1897.

225

us pray the prayer of the Pharisee, *"O God, I thank you that I'm not like the rest of humanity – greedy, dishonest, adulterous ..."*[272] We are self-righteous; it is really only a question of what we are self-righteous about.

We used to stereotype self-righteousness in one phrase: *"Holier-than-thou."* We are all *"holier-than-thou"* except we each define holiness according to our own idiosyncratic preferences, such as *"more-sensitive-than-thou," "brighter-than-thou," "less-hypocritical-than-thou," "more-experienced-than-thou," "less-bigoted-than-thou," "less-rigid-than-thou,"* or *"more-of-a-victim-than-thou."* In subtle and not so subtle ways, each of us is more judge than repentant sinner.

We stop being a judge only when we can claim our proper place among the broken, among God's little ones, the unfaithful and the sinner.

Finally, we must move from speaking about love to actually letting ourselves be loved.

Henri Nouwen uses his own life as an example. For years he went all over the world giving talks about love even while refusing to allow those around him to love him. Only after moving in with the physically handicapped, with people who were not interested in what he had to say about love, did he actually allow himself to be loved.

---

[272] Lk 18:11.

What was true for him is true for most of us. It is far easier for us to speak about love than to let ourselves actually be loved.

In Thomas Aquinas's great work Summa Theologica, he centers on existence itself as the word that can most adequately be applied to God. Existence is the primary value, the fundamental good, one with the very being of God. And since all other beings have their own existence by gift of God, our existence is our primary value and goodness. *"Everything that exists is, as such, good, and has God as its cause."*[273] If we exist — and we cannot cause ourselves into existence — we must have been willed and loved into existence.

God not only creates and sustains every existent being, God also creates every kind of being there is. Every being participates in a hierarchy of goodness and intrinsic value. Each species is good, not only because it exists in the first place, but also because of what it is. Each species brings its own kind of goodness into the world and each species lost would be a loss of goodness. All creation, in all its myriad forms, is existentially good.

Aquinas valued personal reality as the *"most perfect grade of existence"*[274] because it images the *"I am-ness"* of God: life that knows itself and gives itself to the other. This is not some glib speciesism which degrades other kinds of life. It is just an

---

[273] Saint Thomas Aquinas, *Summa Theologica*.
[274] Ibid.

acknowledgment that freedom, intelligence, and love introduce a new splendor of intrinsic goodness and value into the world, which without persons would be bereft of such beauty.

But the existence of personal creatures like human beings also introduces a host of problems to the world. Our peculiar goodness as humans is not only a function of the fact that we exist, but that we exist as a special kind.

We also present a moral goodness to the world since we, with our capacities for intelligence and freedom, are able to know and possess ourselves and consequently choose to become the kind of persons we become.

Evil for Aquinas has no reality in itself. It occurs only as a parasite. Evil appears only because good things exist.

Physical evil is a deficiency or lack in the physical reality of various kinds of beings. Thus a horse might not be fully good as a horse because it is lame. A fig tree is physically evil to the extent that it does not bear the fruit of what it is.

Moral evil, however, is a deficiency or lack in the kind of human being you or I have freely chosen to be. It is a negation of our truth. It is a rejection of our goodness. It is a radical lie about existence.

"*By this is my Father glorified,*" Christ said, "*that you bear much fruit and become my disciples.*"[275] But even when we have

---

[275] Jn 13:8.

glorified the Father by bearing much fruit and becoming Christ's disciples, we still have no right to claim the credit for it as though the work were ours alone.

The grace to carry out the work had first to come to us from God and so the glory is His not ours.

That is why Jesus told the crowds, "*Just so, your light must shine before others, that they may see your good deeds.*" And here, lest they be tempted to attribute those good deeds to themselves, he immediately added, "*and glorify your heavenly Father.*"[276]

This then is the Father's glory, that we should bear abundant fruit and become Christ's disciples, since it is only through God's mercy in the first place that we can become Disciples of Christ. Or as Saint Paul tells us, "*we are His handiwork, created in Christ Jesus for the good works that God has prepared in advance, that we should live in them.*"[277]

# A fresh surprise of love

Few would doubt that God loves us. What is a far greater challenge is to understand and accept the true nature of His love. God's love is beyond measure, it is unconditional, and it is eternal. It is a love full of forgiveness and complete acceptance of our human weaknesses and of our failures.

---

[276] Mt 5:16.
[277] Eph 2:10.

What is also true is that we may never grasp the true depth and meaning of God's love. As with our feeble attempts to know or define God — who is unknowable — we cannot adequately express in human terms the nature of His feelings for all of His creation.

We use words such as love, forgiveness, and acceptance, yet even as we utter them we must summarily recognize their complete inadequacy to convey the incomprehensible.

What we must recognize is that, although we cannot comprehend the true measure of God's love, we are bound by the very life received from Him to love Him in return.

How are we to love God?

Jesus tells us, *"You shall love the LORD, your God, with all your heart, with all your soul, and with all your mind"* and ... and *"You shall love your neighbor as yourself."*[278]

And therein lies the rub. How glibly we confess to loving God. We often say it without thought or feeling. We seldom say it with all of our heart, with all of our soul, and with all of our mind. And we conveniently forget to love our neighbor because we often have issues with loving ourselves.

The commandment to love is like a coin with two sides: one side is love of God and the other side is love of neighbor.

---

[278] Mt 22:37-38.

One coin, two sides. You cannot love God if you hate your neighbor, nor can you love your neighbor without loving God.

What Jesus tells us is that it requires a triple-play: one, you must love God; two, you must love yourself; and three, you must love your neighbors.

But how can you love your neighbor who wishes to do you harm? How do you love those who inflict pain and suffering on others, who perform despicable deeds, or who are instruments of evil?

Consider that each of us was created by God and born into this world from the womb of our mother. A mother loves her child no matter what her child may or may not do. Her love, by her very nature as a mother, is unconditional. She loves her child not for the child's deeds or actions, but for the pure and simple fact that the child is hers. She loves her child because she gave so much of herself in order to produce another living, breathing human being. How much more then must God love us?

We often find it difficult to love others because we are incapable of seeing beyond the surface and not knowing what lies within another's heart, mind, and soul. We see what is exposed, but can only glimpse at what is hidden.

But God sees into our hearts and as Father Ron Rolheiser writes:

*God understands. Crassly put, God isn't stupid! If we,*
*with our limits, can see beyond wound and struggle to*
*a goodness that lies still deeper within a human heart,*
*how much more does God see our goodness, understand*
*our struggles and forgive our weaknesses.*[279]

Throughout the pages of the Bible we are presented with events that speak to us of life and death and life again. They provide us with images of life as we know it now, of a new life that awaits us, and of the fullness of God's love.

A poem written by Rabindranath Tagore expresses this so very well:

*I remember my childhood when the sunrise,*
*like my play-fellow, would burst in to my bedside*
*with its daily surprise of morning;*
*when the faith in the marvelous bloomed*
*like fresh flowers in my heart every day,*
*looking into the face of the world in simple gladness;*
*when insects, birds and beasts, the common weeds,*
*grass and the clouds had their fullest value of wonder;*
*when the patter of rain at night brought dreams*
*from the fairyland, and mother's voice in the evening*
*gave meaning to the stars.*

*And then I think of death,*
*and the rise of the curtain*

---

[279] Fr Ron Rolheiser, *In Exile*, 10th Sunday of Ordinary Time, June 9, 2013, Saint Louis University, The Center for Liturgy.

*and the new morning*
*and my life awakened in its fresh surprise of love.*[280]

I believe that it is that *"fresh surprise of love"* that in truth embodies God's love. If we live our lives loving God and all that surrounds us – even the common weeds, the unlovable, and the despised – then on that new morning we shall awaken to a fresh surprise of love.

# He gave it to me

St. Martin of Tours was a Bishop in the fourth century. Born to a senior officer in the Roman army, he was required to join the army at the age of fifteen. One day, while he was serving in the army, as he was approaching the gates of the city of Amiens, he met a barely clothed man begging for alms in the freezing cold. He immediately stopped and impulsively cut his military cloak in half and shared it with the beggar. That night Martin dreamed of Jesus wearing the half-cloak he had given away and he heard Jesus say to the angels: "*Here is Martin, the Roman soldier who is not baptized; he gave it me.*" Martin's disciple and biographer Sulpicius Severus states that as a consequence of this vision Martin *"flew to be baptized."*[281]

A common and familiar theme presented by Jesus throughout his public ministry was that we must love our neighbor as ourselves and care for the marginalized. One of the

---

[280] Sir Rabindranath Tagore, *Lover's Gift and Crossing # 71*, 1918.
[281] Sulpitius Severus, *On the Life of Saint Martin*.

best examples of this is the parable of the rich man and Lazarus[282] found in the Gospel of Luke. Jesus tells us of a rich man who lived sumptuously while ignoring a poor man called Lazarus who was starving to death at his door. Lazarus died and went to heaven; the rich man was consigned to the netherworld where he was tormented by flames and suffered greatly from thirst. When the rich man pleaded for Lazarus to dip his finger in water and cool his thirst he was told *"My child, remember that you received what was good during your lifetime while Lazarus likewise received what was bad; but now he is comforted here, whereas you are tormented."*[283]

If we are asked to describe our faith, what might immediately come to mind are such things as the creed, church doctrine and dogma, morality, family and community, and our personal relationship with God. And while these are all essential and important elements of faith, they are in many ways focused only on the letter of the law much as the Pharisees, and miss the most important criteria for true discipleship.

Jesus constantly and insistently commands us to feed the hungry, clothe the naked, care for the poor, welcome the stranger, care for the sick, and visit those who are in prison. The importance that Jesus places on caring for the poor and marginalized can be measured by the fact that every tenth line in the New Testament is a direct challenge to care for the poor.

---

[282] Lk 16:19-31.
[283] Lk 16:25.

It should be abundantly clear that Jesus considers acts of mercy and compassion for the poor important as and perhaps even more so than any creed, dogma, or doctrine.

He tells us that when the Son of Man comes, He will judge us by whether we served the least of his brothers and sisters. He calls us to love one another, to see Christ in each other, and to encounter Christ in everyone we meet.

A portion of a poem attributed to Saint Patrick of Ireland called the Lorica[284] conveys the closeness that Christ is to each of us:

*Christ with me, Christ before me, Christ behind me,*
*Christ in me, Christ beneath me, Christ above me,*
*Christ on my right, Christ on my left,*

*Christ when I lie down,*
*Christ when I sit down,*
*Christ when I arise...*

*Christ in the heart of every man who thinks of me,*
*Christ in the mouth of every one who speaks of me,*
*Christ in the eye of every one who sees me,*
*Christ in every ear that hears me.*

Each of us is the body of Christ and, as such we are called to act in his name. So remember whenever you encounter:

---

[284] Attributed to Saint Patrick of Ireland, Also known as "The Deer's Cry" and "St. Patrick's Breastplate."

someone who is hungry and you give them food,
someone who is thirsty, and you give them drink,
a stranger and you welcome them,
someone who is naked and you clothe them,
someone who is sick and you care for them,
someone who is in prison and you visit them

that you are doing it to one of the least and to Christ himself.
And it is for this that you will inherit the kingdom prepared for
you from the foundation of the world.

# About the Author

Charles (Chuck) R. Lanham was ordained into the Permanent Diaconate September 17, 2011. It has been a long and often tortuous road.

Deacon Chuck currently serves the parish of Saint Albert the Great Catholic Community of the Diocese of Reno, Nevada. He is the Director of Adult Faith Formation and Homebound Ministries for the parish, conducts frequent adult faith formation workshops, and is a frequent homilist. He writes a weekly column for the parish bulletin and is a contributor to the Diocesan newspaper. He is also the current president of the Catholic Professionals & Business Group of Reno, NV.

Happily married to Janet for forty-six years, they have two daughters and five grandchildren. He holds undergraduate degrees in History & Political Science, and Business Administration, and a graduate degree in Computer Science. He is a Vietnam Veteran, who served in the U.S. Army for nine years. He has worked at several large computer and software companies, and has founded three startup businesses. He is the author of numerous technical papers and books and currently shares a patent for a remote monitoring device.

He regularly speaks to groups of all ages and sizes and would welcome the opportunity to speak to your group. He can be contacted through his website and blog at

http://www.deaconscorner.org

He lives in Reno, Nevada, just minutes away from the shores of Lake Tahoe; you cannot get much closer to heaven than there.

# Bibliography

What follows is a partial list of books that were referenced when writing this book. While every attempt has been made to list those cited within this manuscript, a few may have inadvertently been missed. I can only offer my deepest apologies for any unintended omissions.

While I have by necessity and faith written this book from a Catholic perspective using primarily Catholic references and sources, numerous books and documents referenced and listed here have been written by authors of other faiths, both Christian and non-Christian, as well as one or two who have professed no faith at all. I believe this should be perfectly acceptable as I have made every attempt to clearly identify any potential divergence.

Please note that the source for every quote can be found in the footnotes. In addition, I have included in the bibliography, books, articles, and web sites that were used in research but not referenced within the pages of the book. They, and all referenced works, are listed for you, the reader, to enjoy as much as I have enjoyed reading them.

*A Free Man's Worship,* by Bertrand Russel. Thomas Mosher. 1903.

*A New Friendship* – The spirituality and Ministry of the Deacon, by Monsignor Edward L. Buelt. Liturgical Press. 2011.

*Because God is Real* – Sixteen Questions, One Answer, by Peter Kreeft. Ignatius Press. 2006.

*Catechism of the Catholic Church* – Second Edition. Libreria Editrice Vaticana. 1994.

*Christian Mystics*, by Matthew Fox. New World Library. 2011.

*Community, Eucharist, and Spirituality*, by Kenan B. Osborne, OFM. Liguori. 2007.

*Compendium* – Catechism of the Catholic Church, United States Conference of Catholic Bishops. Libreria Editrice Vaticana. 2006.

*The Complete C. S. Lewis Signature Classics*, by C. S. Lewis. Harper Collins Publishers. 2007.

*Conversations with God* – An uncommon dialogue, book 1, by Neale Donald Walsch. G. P. Putnam's Sons. 1996.

*Cycling Through the Gospels* – Gospel Commentaries for Cycles A, B, and C, by Jerome J. Sabatowich. Resource Publications. 1992.

*Discernment* – Reading the signs of daily life, by Henri J. M. Nouwen. HarperCollins Publishers. 2013.

*Discourse on Method and Meditation on First Philosophy*, Fourth Edition, by Rene' Descartes, translated by Donald A. Cress. Hackket Publishing Company. 1637, 1998.

*Exodus* – Collegeville Bible Commentary, by Mark S. Smith. Liturgical Press. 2011.

*Fundamentals of the Faith* – Essays in Christian Apologetics, by Peter Kreeft. Ignatius Press. 1988.

*Genesis* – Collegeville Bible Commentary, by Pauline A. Viviano. Liturgical Press. 1985.

*Golda*, by Elinor Burkett. HarperCollins Publishers. 2009.

*Grace for the Moment* – Volume I, by Max Lucado. J. Countryman. 2000.

*Handbook of Christian Apologetics* – Hundreds of Answers to Crucial Questions, by Peter Kreeft & Ronald K. Tacelli. InterVarsity Press. 1994.

*Homilies on the Gospel of St. Matthew*, by St. John Chrysostom. Veritas Splendor Publications. 2012.

*Humbly Submitting to Change* – The Wilderness Experience, by E`yen A. Gardner. Printed Word Publishing. 2010.

*'In the Beginning..'* – A Catholic understanding of the Story of Creation and the Fall, by Pope Benedict XVI, Joseph Ratzinger. William B. Eerdmans Publishing Company. 1986.

*Intimacy*, by Henri J. M. Nouwen. HarperCollins Publishers. 1969.

*Intimacy With God* – Clement of Alexandria, by David Bercot. Scroll Publishing Co. 2012.

*Jacob's Ladder* – Ten steps to truth, by Peter Kreeft. Ignatius Press. 2013.

*Jesus of Nazareth* – from the Baptism in the Jordan to the Transfiguration, by Pope Benedict XVI, Joseph Ratzinger. Libreria Editrice Vaticana. 2007.

*Keys to First Corinthians* – Revisiting the Major Issues, by Jerome Murphy-O'Connor. Oxford University Press. 2009.

*Life of the Beloved* – Spiritual Living in a Secular World, by Henri J. M. Nouwen. The Crossroad Publishing Company. 1992.

*Love Story*, by Erich Segal. Hodder & Stoughton. 1970.

*Lover's Gift and Crossing*, by Sir Rabindranath Tagore. Macmillan and Co. 1918.

*Making All Things New* – An invitation to the Spiritual Life, by Henri J. M. Nouwen. HarperCollins Publishing. 1981.

*Making Choices* – Practical wisdom for everyday moral decisions, by Peter Kreeft. Servant Books. 1990.

*Meditations with Julian of Norwich,* by Brendan Doyle. Bear & Company. 1983.

*Meditations With Meister Eckhart,* by Matthew Fox. Bear & Company. 1981.

*Meister Eckhart* – A Modern Translation, by Raymond B Blakney. Harper & Row, Publishers. 1941.

*Meister Eckhart* – The essential sermons, commentaries, treatises, and defense, translated and introduced by Edmund Colledge, O.S.A. and Bernard McGinn. Paulist Press. 1981.

*Meister Eckhart* – from whom God hid nothing: Sermons, Writings, and Sayings, Meister Eckhart. New Seeds. 2005.

*Meister Eckhart* – Teacher and Preacher, Edited by Bernard McGinn. Paulist Press. 1986.

*New Seeds of Contemplation,* by Thomas Merton. New Directions Publishing. 2007.

*Civil Disobedience,* by Henry David Thoreau. Amazon Digital Services. 1849.

*Out of Solitude* – Three Meditations on the Christian Life, by Henri J. M. Nouwen. Ave Maria Press. 2004.

*Passion for Creation* – The Earth-Honoring Spirituality of Meister Eckhart, by Matthew Fox. Inner Traditions. 2000.

*Pseudo-Dionysius* – The complete works, translation by Colm Luibheid. Paulist Press. 1987.

*Reading the New Testament* – An introduction, Third Edition, by Pheme Perkins. Paulist Press. 2012.

*Sermons of Meister Eckhart*, by Meister Eckhart. Amazon Digital Services. 2010.

*Reading the Old Testament* – An introduction, Second Edition, by Lawrence Boadt, CSP. Paulist Press. 2012.

*Sartor Resartus*, by Thomas Carlyle. Oxford University Press. 1987.

*Silent Hope* – Living with the Mystery of God, by John Kirvan. Sorin Books. 2001.

*Summa Contra Gentiles*, by Saint Thomas Aquinas. Amazon Digital Services. 2010.

*Summa Theologica*, by Saint Thomas Aquinas. Christian Classics. 1981.

*The Catholic Way* – Faith for Living Today, by Bishop Donald W. Wuerl. Doubleday. 2001.

*The City of God*, by Saint Augustine of Hippo, translated by Marcus Dods, D.D. Hendrickson Publishers. 2009.

*The Cloud of Unknowing* – with the Book of Privy Counsel, A new translation by Carmen Acevedo Butcher. Shambhala. 2011.

*The Confessions of Saint Augustine* – 401 AD, translated by Edward Bouverie Pusey. Amazon Digital Services. 2012.

*The Divine Milieu*, by Pierre Teilhard de Chardin. Harper Perennial. 2001.

*The Essential Catholic Survival Guide*: Answers to tough questions about the faith, by the staff of Catholic Answers.

*The Fathers Know Best*: Your essential guide to the teachings of the Early Church, by Jimmy Akin. Catholic Answers. 2010.

*The Heavens Declare the Glory of God* – How the universe provides evidence for the existence of God, by Trent Horn. Catholic Answers Magazine, March/April 2014.

*The Hound of Heaven*, by Francis Thompson. Dodd, Mead and Company. 1926.

*The Inner Voice of Love* – A journey through anguish to freedom, by Henri J. M. Nouwen. Doubleday. 1998.

*The Kingdom of Heaven Within You* – The teachings of Meister Eckhart, Volume 1, translated by C. M. Vega. Amazon Digital Services. 2014.

*The Kingdom of Heaven Within You* – The teachings of Meister Eckhart, Volume 2, translated by C. M. Vega. Amazon Digital Services. 2013.

*The Life of Saint Martin*, by Severus Suplicius. Amazon Digital Services. 2013.

*The Lord of the Rings* – The Hobbit, The Fellowship of the Ring, The Two Towers, The Return of the King, by J.R.R. Tolkien. Del Rey. 1954.

*The Master's Violin*, by Mytle Reed. Grosset & Dunlap Publishers, 1904.

*The New American Bible* – Saint Joseph Edition. Catholic Book Publishing Corp., New York. 1992.

*The New Testament* – The Ignatius Catholic Study Bible, Revised Standard Version, Second Catholic Edition. Ignatius Press. 2000.

*The Phenomenon of Man*, by Pierre Teilhard de Chardin. Harper Perennial. 2002.

*The Return of the Prodigal Son* – A story of homecoming, by Henri J. M. Nouwen. Doubleday. 1994.

*The New Jerome Biblical Commentary*, edited by Raymond E. Brown, S.S., Joseph A. Fitzmyer, S.J., Roland E. Murphy, O.Carm. Prentiss Hall.

*The Perennial Philosophy*, by Aldous Huxley. Harper & Brothers. 1945.

*The Year of Faith* – A Bible Study Guide for Catholics, by Fr. Mitch Pacwa, S.J. Our Sunday Visitor Publishing. 2012.

*To Live is to Love* – Meditations on love and Spirituality, by Ernesto Cardenal. Herder and Herder. 1972.

*Upon This Rock* – St. Peter and the Primacy of Rome in Scripture and the Early Church, by Stephen K. Ray. Ignatius Press. 1999.

*The Word Among Us* – A Catholic devotional magazine. http://www.wau.org.

*10 Books That Screwed Up The World* – And 5 others that didn't help, by Benjamin Wiker, Ph.D. Regnery Publishing. 2008.

*10 Jewels of Christian Mysticism* – A selection of Western Tradition Primary Texts, by Justs Junkulis. Amazon Digital Services. 2013.

## Music

*If Today you hear God's voice, Glory to God* – The Best of David Haas, Volume 4, recorded by David Haas. 2009.

*It's Hard to be Humble*, by Mac Davis. 1980.

*Lookin' for Love*, by Wanda Mallette, Bob Morrison, and Patti Ryan, recorded by Johnny Lee, June 1980.

www.ingramcontent.com/pod-product-compliance
Lightning Source LLC
Chambersburg PA
CBHW071319090426
42738CB00012B/2729